Prefaces

In 1998 John had a back operation and I realised that, trapped as he was, I might at last get the memories out of him that I had always been urging him to write down. He has always hated the past. Only today and tomorrow are important to him, fresh and full of hope, even in old age. I persuaded Martin Farr, now a history don at Newcastle, to start the ball rolling by taping conversations which over the next three years were, as Martin says, redrafted and tweaked right up to press day. In making it manageable I hope I haven't bleached out too much of the original colour.

Julia Henniker, April 2002

This 89,262 word manuscript – reduced to 60,000 words eventually – is the product of over 30 hours of recorded conversations, many more hours recorded, hundreds of pages of correspondence, memoranda and other papers, a long life of service, and a great deal of groaning. In this context, the finished product can hardly be described as excessive. It is not a panygeric, but rather a record in reflection, and one, like so much else, the author has seen as being his duty to undertake. Duty rather than enthusiasm has perhaps been his driving motivation; to be both effusive and self-effacing is to present problems for an assistant. Just how problematic remains to be seen. To paraphrase one of his anecdotes (page 40), if the title remains when the author has finished his redrafting, the assistant will have done all right.

Martin Farr, Wareside, February 1999

Chronology

1916	Born
1922	Wellesley House, Broadstairs, Kent (preparatory school)
1928	Stowe School
1934	Trinity College, Cambridge
1938	Foreign Office
1940	Enlisted, Essex Regiment
1940	Second Lieutenant, Second Battalion, Rifle Brigade (Prince Consort's Own)
1942	Wounded, Seventh Armoured Division, Eighth Army, Libya
1942	Lieutenant
1943	Captain
1943	Parachuted into Bosnia
1944	Parachuted into Serbia
1944	Major
1945	Military Cross
1945-1946	Second Secretary, British Embassy, Belgrade
1946-1948	Assistant Private Secretary to Secretary of State for Foreign Affairs
1946	Married Margaret Osla Benning
1948	Assistant Head of European Recovery Department Mutual Aid (Marshall Plan)
1950-1952	Head of Chancery, British Embassy, Buenos Aires
1952	Counsellor, Foreign Office
1953-1960	Head of Personnel, Foreign Office
1956	Companion of the Most Distinguished Order of St Michael and St George
1960	Commander of the Royal Victorian Order
1960-1962	HM Ambassador, Jordan
1962-1966	HM Ambassador, Denmark

Painful extractions

Photographed in Cairo at the studio of Jean Weinberg, about 1942.

Painful extractions

Looking back at a personal journey

John Henniker

THORNHAM BOOKS
2002

© *John Henniker 2002*

*Published in June 2002
in an edition of 300 casebound copies,
and reprinted as a paperback in 2007*

ISBN *978-1-84753-525-2*

Cover portrait by John Ward, 1978

*Thornham Books
Red House, Thornham Magna, Eye, Suffolk* IP23 8HH

Contents

Prefaces *page 7*
Chronology *page 8*

ONE Childhood, 1916 to 1934 *page 11*
TWO Cambridge, 1934 to 1937 *page 28*
THREE Germany, 1936 *page 33*
FOUR The Foreign Office, 1938 to 1940 *page 37*
FIVE Going to war, 1941 and 1942 *page 46*
SIX Yugoslavia, 1943 to 1945 *page 58*
SEVEN Belgrade, 1945 and 1946 *page 78*
EIGHT Ernie, 1946 to 1948 *page 86*
NINE Os, 1948 to 1960 *page 100*
TEN The Foreign Office, 1938 to 1968 *page 103*
ELEVEN Personnel, 1953 to 1960 *page 108*
TWELVE Jordan, 1960 to 1962 *page 123*
THIRTEEN Denmark, 1962 to 1966 *page 132*
FOURTEEN The British Council, 1968 to 1972 *page 140*
FIFTEEN Recuperating, 1972 to 1980 *page 151*
SIXTEEN The final chapter *page 157*

Appendix *page 167*

1965	Knight Commander of the Most Distinguished Order of St Michael and St George
1966-1967	Group Chairman, Civil Service Commission
1967-1968	Assistant Under-Secretary (Africa)
1968-1972	Director-General, British Council
1972-1978	Director, Wates Foundation
1973-1990	Trustee, City Parochial Foundation
1974	Death of Osla
1974-1986	Member of Council, University of East Anglia
1974-1986	Lay member, Mental Health Review Tribunal (Broadmoor)
1976	Married Julia Marshall Poland
1978	Commencement of Thornham development
1979-1990	Governor, Cripplegate Foundation
1979-1983	Member, Parole Board
1980	Succeeded his father as eighth Baron Henniker
1980-1987	Deputy Chairman, Toynbee Hall
1982-1990	Governor, Stowe School
1983-1990	Chairman, Suffolk Community Alcohol Services
1985-1988	Vice-President, Suffolk Trust for Nature Conservation
1985-1988	President, Suffolk and North Essex Institute of Management
1985-1990	Chairman, Intermediate Treatment Fund
1985-1991	Chairman, Suffolk Rural Housing Association
1986-1990	Vice-President, National Association Victims Support Schemes
1986-1992	Lay Canon, St Edmundsbury Cathedral
1986-1993	President, Community Council for Suffolk
1988	Liberal Democrat Spokesman on Environmental Affairs
1989	President, Suffolk Agricultural Association
1989	Hon. Doctor of Civil Law, University of East Anglia
1993	Hon. Doctor of Laws, New England College, Henniker, New Hampshire
2000	Opening of Walled Garden

ONE

Childhood, 1916 to 1934

It is perhaps best to start at the beginning, which for me was 19th February 1916. I was born at my grandparents' house at 54 Upper Brook Street, Mayfair, where my mother and her brother and sister had themselves been brought up. Probably to enhance the drama of this event it was always alleged there was that night a Zeppelin raid on London, but nobody was ever able to confirm this.

My first memories are of Burghclere, near Newbury, driving along with my mother in the smart trap on golden days, then sitting on glorious Beacon Hill, a dream of cowslips, with my father and his legendary colleagues from the Royal Flying Corps: de Crespigny, the Squadron commander, Maurice Newnham, John Williams a co-pilot, with whom he was soon to make a record-breaking flight to Australia. For a small boy it was heaven.

Another memory and I am off with grandfather to track down the fox which had taken some of the hens; and then a most frightening shot of me shaking apples from a tree and seeing a pony start to eat them, then charging in to save them, and being kicked over by the pony and looking up at it in sheer terror till I was rescued by a frightened mother. It was not a typical incident. I was happy. For Nanny Payne I could do no wrong. No overtones of worry about what job my father was to get when the war ended came through to me.

The next memories are of Budleigh Salterton, on the south coast of Devon, where my grandparents had built a house near the golf course at the top of a steep hill. My grandfather played golf, was captain of the club, and won veterans' trophies. The garden was full of good things: apple trees, including some Lady Hennikers; fruit and vegetables, and my Granny always on her knees weeding. For us children it was perfect: we had the sea, we were spoiled by my grandparents' friends, and the couple – the Legges – the cook and butler who looked after them. Even now I still feel the ecstasy of the start of the holidays when I hear the gulls calling as they did from the top of the police station in Budleigh; at Budgen's, the grocer, with the Wiltshire Bacon mmn, who always had some treat for us. Fragments of memory. All was sunlight. But the sea was cold.

When I was born my mother was 21, my father 31, and for two years had been in France as Adjutant to a squadron of the Royal Flying Corps. Until Dick joined me I was centre of the stage in a female household. When my father came back from the war my nose was put out of joint and so was his, which led to constant battles of will throughout my life.

Much as I loved my mother – and I was closer to her than was my brother – she always took my father's side when I was under scrutiny. She was born in November on one side or the other of Guy Fawke's Night, though I could never remember which. She was my grandfather's favourite, but when she was born my grandmother was said to have been – quite unjustifiably – so disappointed that she was not a boy that she turned her face to the wall and refused to think of a name for her. Finally she settled at the last moment for only a nickname: Molly. Nonetheless, there were, though it was not immediately apparent, considerable advantages. Much was hoped of the older children: very little of my mother, though my grandfather always loved her dearly.

My grandfather was my model. He often came to my rescue and did not as a doctor feel that my father's constant criticism of me was wise. He – Sir Robert William Burnet – was at the time at the height of his career as a physician in the West End. I came to love him and my grandmother Bessie very much. The marriage was strangely improbable, for he remained unrepentantly Scottish, with a broad accent, and an unrelenting honesty with fashionable ladies who enjoyed the dramas of their illnesses. He had very few social or material ambitions, and his career would be a happy combination of ability and luck.

He was a son of the manse, and was born in 1851 at Huntly, Aberdeenshire, where his father was minister. While at university, my grandfather attracted the attention of his professor, Sir George Clark. Clark was a royal physician, and on the completion of my grandfather's clinical studies summoned his pupil south to help him with his royal duties. Sir George persuaded my grandfather to go on Lord Lorne and Princess Beatrice's royal tour of Canada, and he never looked back. In 1856 he became honorary physician to the Prince of Wales, and so he remained until the latter became King as George V. He remained physician to the royal household until 1919, when he had to retire, through illness. He was disappointed, but was 68, so it was hardly premature. He recovered completely, and, though he never worked again, he seemed to me to have a totally happy life in which golf played a very important part. I remember him first when he and Granny lived at Grey Court, Burghclere which they had built, and where we went to live at the Malt House immediately after my father came back from the war. Grey Court represented a more spacious life than they could now afford. In the end it was sold to friends – the Behrends – for whom Stanley Spencer later painted the famous chapel.

Granny was everything a grandmother should be: a haven from the improving tendencies of one's parents. Granny thought, strangely, that I was entirely satisfactory, provided good food and comfort, and was enormously proud of my every achievement, however trivial. Grandmother was in many ways quite the opposite of my grandfather, which puzzled me. I never knew how she – comfortable, sophisticated and pleasure-loving – could ever have come close enough to the rather home-spun, craggy, and simple Scottish boy my grandfather must have been ever to get married to him. But happen it did, and the result was almost idyllically happy.

Granny very much enjoyed the social life and comfort, and had sufficient income to provide for both. She towed my grandfather rather unwillingly into the social world, and, as it greatly helped his professional career, this caused no friction whatsoever. Granny always seemed to me to have stepped straight out of the Forsyte family: a vast concourse of cousins, Coles, Fords, Morleys. A sort of tribe. She was, in my memory, surrounded by large, affable, prosperous men, who had large houses in Streatham and did arcane things in the City. Uncle Bill, Uncle Taffy, Cousin Basil; to a small boy inhabiting a peaceful Valhalla, they were friendly and generous, but their world remained totally mysterious to me. Even today these large dark men go marching on: a brood of Fords, Duke Hussey, Robin Ferrers, even. Dick and I we were miniature by comparison. Incidentally, Marmaduke Hussey's *Chance Governs All*, published in 2001, gives a good account of my grandmother's family.

After grandfather died, Granny moved down into the town nearly opposite my old Mecca, the Wiltshire Bacon Man, and changed with changing times. Whenever I needed comfort or a rest I went to stay with Granny, and she never failed me. I always left Budleigh Salterton with my tail up sure I could face the world. The curtain came down not long before the war with a sad concourse of large, but older and prosperous dark men, gathered in Brookwood Cemetery to wish Gran farewell. These cemeteries seem to me sad and gloomy as a last resting-place, and I was always sad that Gran ended up there, though my mother did make a little memorial to remember both her parents in Thornham church. Even that is not quite the place: I would rather think of them together on the hill at Budleigh, when we were all so happy together. Dear Gran: until the war, I used to sneak off occasionally to see her lovely little grave lying almost anonymously amongst so many.

My grandmother's hopes were much satisfied by her elder daughter Elizabeth, and her son Jack – Jacko. Brought up in a family of able and active men, the male had the benefit of every doubt and had difficulty in doing any wrong. Jacko was physically akin to the larger, darker clan of my grandmother's family: in danger of running to fat and of enjoying the luxury of prosperity.

I have always felt that if a family's character comes from a bank of genes, Aunt Elizabeth and I drew on the same account. I always had a fellow feeling for her. Elizabeth, though dark, was much more like my spare and sandy-haired grandfather. Unlike most of my family, she was slight, wiry, enormously energetic, sharp-witted, and prepared for any amount of hard work wherever battle was joined. From my grandmother she inherited, I think, her outlook on life to a greater extent: she loved people, and loved to be surrounded by lots of them.

Her particular virtue was a desire to excel at whatever she might do. At one time she became a very real pundit on the art of quilting – not a pursuit likely to lead to fame and fortune. Somewhere I think she had my grandmother's feeling that women should challenge men on their own ground. She was the joy of governesses who gave her all they had, leaving my

My father in 1916.

mother to find her own, rather self-effacing way.

For someone brought up in a strictly conventional atmosphere, she had a curious streak of unconventionality. A little maverick peeped out from under her hem. She was interested in everything that went on around her and for a time she was a sharp-tongued short-skirted feminist, constantly to be found reacting against the establishment. She expressed every new idea with enthusiasm, even when they were not exactly fashionable, though her respect for her male-ordered world did not allow her to carry her zeal past the point of propriety. She was with the suffragettes, though not so far as to lead her to the conclusion that man's primacy in the family was in doubt. My first memory of her was after a visit to Ireland, where she had been to see what really happened in those troubled times. This led to a period of passion for Sinn Fein and the freedom of the Irish. I think Elizabeth is the origin of my own radicalism. Of all my relations, she was the one I thought I was most like.

Aunt Elizabeth's friends were often respectable, but nevertheless included avant-garde clerics and their bluestocking wives. Bloomsbury or the East End attracted her much more than did Mayfair, though the conventions remained fairly important. She eventually married in 1924, a little late in life for a girl of those days, but perhaps she was more articulate, more inquisitive than was expected of girls at a time when a more submissive and quiet attitude was expected. Guy Hake, an architect and intellectual, was exactly right. He was wholly respectable, but had that streak of unconventionality that appealed to her.

Guy came from a rather *outré* family – the Hakes and the Rossettis – who were artists, friends of the Pre-Raphaelites. Guy enjoyed that world. They lived in Clifton in the academia of Bristol and she took to it like a duck to water and served and loved him throughout their marriage. When Guy retired they moved to Yarcombe in Devon. They had prepared a house for their retirement, and I remember my first visit; a magic moment in my life. We slept in a caravan in the garden with a stream tinkling by, kingcups in the fields next to the river. One has but few special memories in this life, and this remains to me the most vivid.

When Guy died a light went out, and the remainder of Elizabeth's life was spent being proud of Andrew and his family. To her joy, he went into the church. We used to gently tease her that she wanted Andrew to be a bishop, but he too, had her penchant for the unconventional, with much the same strong social convictions, which had held her back.

Though he did not become a bishop, Elizabeth's son Andrew nevertheless made a great contribution as an important social worker and thinker, who was on Archbishop Runcie's Commission, which produced the controversial report *Faith in the City* in 1985.

My uncle Jacko was a great success without any visible accomplishments. Jacko may have been I fear, shamefully spoiled. He could do no wrong and the best and most expensive education had to be his. At an early age he showed some originality by becoming enormously attracted to the police; not that he wanted to be one, but he loved their company and their jokes and for years the kitchen of Upper Brook Street always tended to be full of his policemen friends. This fell away when he went on to Eton, but it left its mark.

Jacko fulfilled the criteria by which Etonians are so often judged: making friends. He was for all his life a man's man, enjoying pubs and clubs, with the latest joke always at his fingertips. At Eton he was not particularly gifted either at games or at work, but nonetheless had a glittering career; he was in Monarch, but strained his heart slightly rowing, he was a huge success in Pop, where his rather fruity, and for a boy, sophisticated sense of humour gave him a special position. His friends – Freeman Thomas (later Lord Willingdon), Eddy Naylor-Leyland (his best friend and later my godfather), George Naylor-Leyland (his younger brother) and many others, became rich with golden fortunes.

The war did him no service. He joined the Royal Fusiliers, but the heart strain he had had at Eton made him unfit for the front and he was shipped off to the United States to try his hand at recruiting, a task for which his earthy humour and male gregariousness seemed admirably suited. This, I think, had the disastrous effect of encouraging a taste for drink. He seldom drank steadily, and was for years often totally disciplined and abstemious. If he had one drink, however, he was away and could not stop until some disaster struck. I remember once he went on until he fell downstairs and broke an arm. He got apparently good jobs: once he was employed by an American millionaire, a Mr. Kelly, who was prospecting for oil in Colombia. We were in North Wales, and met him, off one of those marvellous floating castles of the White Star Line. Kelly was a Pasha, distributing largesse but then, while on leave, the bubble burst. There was no oil. Kelly shot himself.

Others helped and got Jacko jobs; he did them well, often for several years, but no firm can stand an alcoholic on the rampage, and in the end he always had to go. I remember one awful night when we were quite young. He took my brother and me to the Ivy. He was immensely generous, but he had a drink, and then he was off. We died of shame. He stood drinks to everyone, shouted his bonhomie to one and all, and got wilder and wilder. I cannot remember how we got away. To attempt to moderate him was like trying to stop Niagara.

Jacko was an excellent golfer and in many ways very disciplined. He kept his handicap low, but he had no intellectual interests and conviviality was his solace. He retired when not more than 50 because his heart was getting too bad and with the coming of the war he was ageing fast. He became a welcome guest at home – and not long afterwards he died at the Red House. It was a sad life. He had many virtues, but somehow his gifts, his expensive education, the love and care he had had, left him incomplete, and somehow quite without real purpose.

There is one other relation for whom I felt a strong affection, that was the brother of Alice Cuffe, my paternal grandmother: Uncle Ham – Hamilton Agmondisham, Earl of Desart, who came from Kerry. He had a distinguished career after marrying a Lascelles, a family which provided many wives for the British aristocracy. He became Attorney General and among other things prosecuted in the trial of Oscar Wilde and was I think sympathetic to him. The papers were lost in a fire when Desart Court was burnt down in the Troubles. He came to stay with us in North Wales when we were very young and I loved him. He was a dear man full of strength and kindness and he used to tell us of going to sea at some fantastically early age, and at 14 was in charge of a ship's boat and its crew of six men. Quite a command for a little boy. He always did excellently well and when he came to stay with us joined in our games, in particular helping me to build the house we had made of bracken at Rhewl House. He told us too of the time when he and Lord Plunkett agreed on the settlement of the Irish problem, and then how Plunkett ratted. He was himself I think tolerant of nationalists and the youngest brother of that family was an ardent nationalist, wearing a kilt and playing bagpipes. I loved him dearly and never saw him

left:
*Gug and Mum,
5th December 1914.*

*below:
Myself (left) with
Dick at Risby,
April 1921.*

again, but I remember him vividly as someone who could share the childhood of little boys, and enjoyed my little black hens as much as I did. He was related to the Verneys and was a highly educated and gentle man with whom I am happy to have some real connection and to share some of his ideals. His daughter, Lady Sybil Lubbock, wrote his life in *A Page from the Past* published in 1936, and his grand-daughter Iris Origo wrote of their family and life in Ireland at Desart Court in her famous book *Images and Shadows*. His brother the fourth Earl of Desart whom Uncle Ham succeeded as fifth Earl, was less successful and married Jewish money – Bishopshymer – to shore up the family finances.

In their differing ways, the Hennikers and the Burnets straddled London society. My maternal grandfather was associated with George V, my paternal grandfather with Edward VII, and my father was a page to Queen Victoria. Politically the Burnets were of a more progressive disposition. Sir Robert was a longstanding friend and physician too of his fellow Scot, Sir Henry Campbell-Bannerman, who was Liberal leader and then Prime Minister.

Cultural parallels were less obvious. The Burnets were part of the world described by Galsworthy in *The Forsyte Saga*; the Hennikers were more at home in the novels of Thomas Hardy. Indeed, my great uncle Arthur lived in what seemed to be a *ménage à trois* with the writer and his own wife Aunt Florence. Florence was the daughter of Lord Houghton and the sister of Lord Crewe and was a close friend of Florence Nightingale. She was a spirited woman who in 1896 became President of the Royal Society of Women Journalists. A correspondence of Hardy and Florence was published recently (*One Rare Woman*, Thomas Hardy's letters to Florence Henniker, edited by Evelyn Hardy and F. B. Pinion, 1972).

When my father returned from the war, we went to live at Risby, near Bury St Edmunds. After first seeking to become Bursar of New College, Oxford, he took up duties as Land Agent to Lord Mostyn, at his estate in North Wales. Life was not in all respects an improvement. My beloved nanny was replaced by a rather frightening fearful Latvian, Miss Von Jacobs, who, despite believing I was bright enough, regularly averred: "He haf no talent". "Jaky" no doubt regarded this as a reason to swing her whip, a notion she unfortunately took literally. My mother was not best pleased that the *émigré* governess she employed saw fit to whip her charges. In other respects I continued as before, and no doubt as my father expected. I first played football, aged about five, with a girl called Marcia, and on kicking the ball for the first time brought on a double hernia which required surgery on Aunt Illy's kitchen table in London, the after effects of which I enjoyed enormously, one of which was the present of a horse on wheels.

The Mostyn family never made us feel very welcome, though Clementine Mostyn, almost our next-door neighbour in Rhewl, became my mother's closest friend, so intimate that it totally relieved the loneliness she had felt on being banished to North Wales from London. I don't think either of my parents liked living there much, but they became very busy with trying to create and improve a local ladies' hockey team who often came to the house and were rather embarrassed to be our friends, but soon they produced a number of women's internationals who played for Wales. My mother and father got about as best they could in a rather isolated area in various forms of transport. My mother had, as far as I can remember, a Clyno and drove it intrepidly over the Welsh hills; its brakes tended to give way and did so once going down the very steep hill into Hollywell, the next-door village. Dick and I often accompanied our parents in the dicky, which were the two little seats behind the driver. We were often freezing but full of excitement at what lay before us. We went regularly to St Asaph, the home of the Archbishop of Wales to learn dancing with the archbishop's two grandsons, Gerald and Geoffrey. We boys always danced together and never – even by chance – saw anything of a girl. We went occasionally to visit the two sons of the neighbouring parson in the next village and played with them. Occasionally we motored forth more bravely to a mysterious and lonely beach full of exciting barrels and other flotsam that had come from passing ships, or occasionally going eastward to Hawarden where descendants of Gladstone still lived and where I always fell over and ended the visit covered with blood.

Once a year we would go to the theatre in the Mostyn's car and once a year Dick would automatically be sick over the chauffeur's polished gaiters and we would have to return home and miss the pantomime. Somewhere between the two there lived a judge called Bankes to whose son I later bowled at prep school. We went too sometimes to Prestatyn for rather gruesome holidays, or to a grand house in Colwyn Bay inhabited by Watson Hughes, a rich Liverpudlian merchant with a beautiful, distant, and disdainful daughter. We also visited the Trevor Eatons, or Lady Bates, who looked to me like a witch and taught my mother Mah Jong. Further afield was Nantclwyd, where my uncle Jacko's closest friend from Eton, Edward Naylor-Leyland, lived. He was my godfather and a constant provider of marvellous birthday presents until he suddenly married a penny-pinching Frenchwoman, when the presents ceased to come. It was, however, a beautiful place though saddened by the death of at least one son in the war. Occasionally we visited some cousins descended from the second marriage of the first Lord Henniker's daughter who married a Welshman, and greatly enjoyed getting wet and filthy building dams with her.

On the whole, I think my parents were glad to leave Mostyn. My father, after a series of interviews, was appointed by Willie Mackenzie, who had built most of the French railways and was reputed to be a tough taskmaster, to be Agent at Fawley Court and the regatta course at Henley and Temple Island, which he owned. My father, however, got on well with Mackenzie who had the habit, if his car passed a pheasant in a field, of getting out and shooting it. He took on as his Assistant Agent, David Gordon, a splendid rugger player with the London Scottish, and the future Lord Aberdeen.

We lived happily in Henley next door to the grammar school and Dick made many friends while I was away at prep school, mainly among the girls of Henley. There in the first holidays I was given a brand new bike and rode boldly out of the house onto the road where I immediately ran into a car, going over the bonnet and doing permanent damage to my nose.

Henley was great fun. I had my pony from North Wales, which grew fatter and lazier on the lush grass beside the Thames. We belonged to a young people's club, played hockey and a bit of football. We explored bits of the Fawley Estate, where I eventually met the Birds whose son Tom became my successful and very gallant commander in the Rifle Brigade and won many decorations. There were many people of our age and constant activity and tennis parties, so that we went off at the end of the holidays for a much needed rest at school.

There were few girls in our lives, but Jane Drummond was a constant and rather beautiful exception. There were the Hoopers at Harpston and the Robinsons up the hill, both with beautiful daughters. The Hamiltons lived at Henley Park and were all vigorous and active competitors with whom we often got up cricket teams and even a rugby XV to play in the holidays. I loved it and was sorry when public school loomed up and interfered and cricket and everything else started to become much more serious and nerve-wracking. Equally I loved my prep school, Wellesley House. I was very competitive and enjoyed any sort of competition at which I was good enough to do well. I was in the cricket XI and played with George and John Mann. George was always the leader and eventually captained England. It was with them as their guest that I was invited to Lords for the Eton and Harrow match, a day full of distant idols at which I saw a related Ford bowl out Eton until he almost broke down under the strain, and the recent CIGS Lord Bramall bolting along a distant boundary to take a quite glorious catch for Eton. Terence Rattigan and Lord Rothschild opened for Harrow and batted sparkingly. It was a very satisfying day and I longed to be one of them but was still too young. Parties went on and my brother Dick and Sherman Stonor made life difficult for me by hiding behind the sofa making sucking noises whenever I tried to get somewhere with Jane.

Father's time at Henley came to an end when my uncle Charles invited him to go back and help him to keep the Estate running at Thornham. We accepted at once, but what was now the Agent's house, the Red House, was not ready for occupation without quite a lot of work to be done. This was just what my mother had wanted and she immediately started laying plans. Meanwhile we had to find a house to rent for a short time and it happened that Rosie Douglas Hamilton, the last and most recently married sister of the Kerrison family, lent us her nice house in Brome. Most of the Kerrisons were dead but one had known my father well and had married a well-known local snob who was known as Hymn Number 547, *Forever with the Lord*, and was seldom seen abroad without a peer in tow. It was a delightful place to live and we soon settled in.

My father enjoyed the work, knew many of the people who worked on the Estate, which with the continuance of the agricultural depression was steadily running down. The Estate, nevertheless, still had seven gamekeepers and the shoot with whom my father, and occasionally uncle Charles regularly shot. There were three cowmen, workshops and a sawmill in the Estate yard. My mother immediately threw herself into overseeing the admirable herd of Red Polls on the park. The shoot was let to a friendly group of London businessmen who came throughout the season, and shot reasonably well, though after lunch they tended to be less accurate.

It was a life, which from the start appealed to Dick and me. Uncle Charles bought us guns and we were sent out regularly, with one of the keepers; sometimes Harry Grass, who married a local girl and went on to become Lord Mountbatten's head keeper at Broadlands and one of the best known in the country.

I loved the place from the start, and I vaguely began to know that when my father died, I might have to take it over, though there was absolutely no sign of any break in the clouds that settled over it after my grandfather died. The main house was still let to Lady Marr who regularly entertained friends such as the Hughes who had been tenants after my grandfather died. They usually had a stain, however slight, on their escutcheon, which was normally no more than a slightly difficult divorce. Even then we knew that the family would not for much longer be able to keep on Thornham Hall and plans for its future were discussed with the likelihood that some part of it at least would have to be pulled down. My uncle Charles, who was a very sweet man, felt keenly that his obligations to his family would never really allow him to settle there, but he kept an elder brother's eye on all the family and did his best to help. He got on reasonably well with my father, but tended to treat him as a slightly irresponsible younger brother. Victor, who had recently married the widow of a former clerical colleague, returned with an excellent cook to the rectory at Thornham Magna.

I always loved the Estate, but had no proprietary feelings about it for it never occurred to me that I could ever possibly afford to keep it up. Shooting, walking, bird watching and getting to know every corner of it took all my time. We had a happy home life but, apart from outdoor activity, there was very little for Dick and me to do. The area was sparsely inhabited and though I was very rarely invited to dances, more often than not I found that I would have to take someone considerably older than me, often a friend of my mother's. I tended to tread on her toes, and was, sad to say, very bored, though I tried to keep the party going. Dick firmly made it clear that he never went to dances, except on one occasion when he was invited to the Stainton's at Henley in my place when I was having my appendix out. He had to take secret dancing lessons in Ipswich before he accepted the invitation, where he met Nancy, his future wife.

I always had in my mind a hope that I might one day be able to do something that would keep the Estate going, but at that time it seemed a very distant hope. Just to be closely involved in its future seemed all I could expect. I felt that all I could possibly afford would be just to keep it going.

I went off to Stowe while the family was at Fawley. Public school was a very different proposition from what I was used to. I had been very successful and had had a happy time at Wellesley House, my prep school at Broadstairs, on the Isle of Thanet. I was a leading Bugger. I led a team of "bug hunters" who caught and dissected various insects. We were called "The Buggers", and corridors outside the Headmaster's study would reverberate to my shrill command: "BUGGERS FALL IN!" I had tremendous pillow fights with the boy in the next door bed, who eventually turned into Viscount Leverhulme, and used to tell me about his grandfather's successes at Port Sunlight. Lever went on to Eton; my father originally had me down for Eton, but the fees at Stowe were £10 a term cheaper, so my brother and I went there. I was less happy at Stowe, and may have had a premonition that that would be the case. I loved Wellesley House, and cried when it came to an end. I was no longer to be a big fish in a small pond.

By most things I am rather daunted, but Stowe was in general a deep disappointment. I have always felt that I was not fully educated there, and Stowe never added very much to my wisdom. I was deputy head boy – second to Laddie Lucas, the golfer, and future Battle of Britain fighter ace. The masters were not much good, and one of the few who was was sacked for drinking.

The ethos was progressive, but pupils were ironically seldom extended intellectually, or in any other way for that matter. It was a new school, and everything was being pioneered. J. F. Roxburgh, the school's first headmaster was at the cutting edge of what then constituted the *avant garde* in teaching. He made a great thing about knowing all the pupils' names. Roxburgh always struck me as being a lonely giant surrounded by pigmy masters: a cedar tree underneath which few other things could grow.

Roxburgh was delighted when I entered the Foreign Office, and particularly with the publicity it brought the school. My year was also a good vintage for war heroes. In addition to Laddie Lucas, my fellow pupils also included Leonard Cheshire, David Niven and Noel Annan. I loved Noel, who came up a year later than me. I was head of the house next door to Noel's and we got to know each other very well. Throughout his life he was always the same. Whenever I saw him we quickly got back to our boyhood relationship. I always wished that when I left Stowe I had followed Noel who made proper use of Stowe's stronger intellectual influences.

Noel was taken up by a much younger master and his wife, who introduced him to a wider range of intellectual problems. They were all matters which interested me but somehow never came my way: the Spanish Civil War, and the menace of the USSR and Nazi Germany. I somehow was never encouraged to think about them. At that time John Cornford became a steady friend and we played golf on the Stowe course and enjoyed it; it came as a great surprise when suddenly at the beginning of the next term, John turned up looking positively scruffy and steadily became more so as he moved towards the communist party. There was no longer any talk of golf; life was altogether too earnest. I missed him, as there was no one else near my standard at golf, or for that matter intellectually. He eventually went to fight in the Spanish Civil War and got killed. His mother, Frances Cornford, wrote a famous poem, among others: *O fat white woman whom nobody loves ...*

Noel became a great figure when he got to Cambridge and became Dean of King's at an early age. He was an easy companion but never quite knew where – politically – he came to rest. But I loved him and that didn't matter. He seemed to mix orthodoxy with a certain iconclasm about society. But he remained respectable. I was very sorry when he died recently, and I was unable to get in touch with his wife. He was kind, particularly to an old friend of ours who developed epilepsy at Cambridge and never let his busy official life interfere with that friendship.

Stowe ended on a sour note. I lost my place in the final rugby XV in the last match against Oundle, and in which Stowe beat Oundle for the first time. I played in the match before against the Old Stoics and felt I had done pretty well. Noel had earlier established his position in the team, but it came as a terrible shock to me in the last practice before the match that I was going to be left out, especially as my parents had come to see the match. I really couldn't believe it and there was quite a small rebellion in the back row of the scrum when to my dismay, Goldsmith led a little protest. But it was even worse when someone who had never played in the team before – and had no ambition to do so – was put in in my place.

I never knew how this could have happened, or why none of my special friends such as Mike Ling protested. I heard afterwards it was because one of the rugger masters had taken the afternoon off to teach me the art of goal kicking and after two abortive shots with a very wet ball, I suggested to Laddie Lucas, the Captain, it would be better to let somebody else have the next shot. I went to the notice board to check that my name was not on the list, and hot tears ran down my cheeks. I then decided that I couldn't watch the match and quickly put my name down to work at the Stowe settlement in the East End – the Pineapple. It was a bitter ending to my last term, though I captained my house team when we won the cup.

TWO

Cambridge, 1934 to 1937

I went up to Cambridge in the autumn of 1934, and entered Trinity, then as now the best of all the Cambridge colleges, and where my grandfather had been before me. Some of my peers hunted; I shot. I was not much into societies, with the exception of the Pitt Club, a dining club, which continues to this day, nor could it be said that I had much success with women. I had to wait until the war was over to learn anything about that subject.

One of the great joys I found at Cambridge was in meeting people who were not from the same school or house as me. For this reason the old Etonians seemed to have a hard time of it, since they were by now thoroughly bored by the same routines and the same people in the same sort of atmosphere as they found at Cambridge.

Early on I met Steven Runciman, a much older figure, by 13 years, and at that time a don who lived on the same staircase as two of my friends. Steven was totally reliable, but also a little unorthodox, and had an unusual taste for introducing rather simple schoolboys, such as myself, to the ramifications of life. With him one had grown-up conversation about people and what they were up to. He seemed to have regarded this as one of the responsibilities of being a don. There were no damaging effects from this, often very much the contrary. For one thing, I learnt what homosexuality was, knowledge which became particularly useful when I came to run the Personnel department of the Foreign Office.

When Noel arrived next year at Cambridge I knew that he might interest Steven, and my first attempt at giving a lunch party in college was to introduce them because I knew they would be each others' equal and I am glad that they were always friends.

Another real friend was Anthony O'Hagan. He lived in Suffolk, which explained our friendship. Towards the end of his time at Cambridge he had some sort of breakdown and suddenly lost his memory. He recovered from that and later went with me to learn German in Munich. While we were there he asked me, because I spoke better German than he, to interpret for him the observations of the psychiatrist from whom he was receiving treatment, an Austrian, Dr. Bumke. This was not a very successful enterprise for the very simple reason that the best clinical results are hardly likely to be achieved with psychiatric treatment conducted through an interpreter in a language in which the interpreter is not fluent. Dr. Bumke asked me, "Does he hear voices?" and I asked Anthony, "Do you hear voices?". Anthony thought for a while. Then he said, "Yes, I do hear voices". It was perfectly clear that he was saying whatever was expected of him.

When Anthony's father died he did not succeed to the O'Hagan title, but for some family reason took the name of Strachey in 1938. Anthony was by that time working as Assistant Private Secretary to Princess Margaret. Later on in London, Osla and I used to see him and his wife Mary. The next awful thing we heard was that Anthony, for reasons I have never known, and while he was still Margaret's equerry, got up, walked out of the room and shot himself.

It was as a result of his nervous breakdown at Cambridge that I damaged our relationship during the war. Because of the emotional stress to which one was inevitably exposed in working with resistance movements in the Balkans, I expressed doubts, via a telegram, as to the wisdom of his joining my mission on the Bulgarian border in 1944. My concern was in exposing him to unnecessary strains: he was, frankly, quite unsuitable: the worst possible person to send there. In that area one was regarded intermittently, when one was not obviously useful, as the representative of a foreign power, which was hostile to communism, the political creed of those which one had been sent to help. I feared then, and still do, that perhaps I had been right and that SOE had possibly not helped by showing, in their usual idiotic way, my telegram to Anthony. SOE always leaked like an old sieve. In any event, they appeared to pay no attention whatever to what I had said, and Anthony quickly arrived to take up the post about which I had expressed misgivings.

David Stirling was another friend, though I was a much closer friend of his brother Hugh. David became famous for founding the SAS, his own private army, and a refuge from the conformity of the services. I was not surprised that he did. Even at Cambridge he was unsafe to be with. To go around with David as an undergraduate would mean fights with the proctors. Whenever he behaved well, it was obvious that his mother was about to visit.

Eddie Tomkins was also with me, and close to me, at Trinity. Eddie lived a good, straightforward, respectable life, doing his jobs as well as he could and not trying or succeeding in investing his life with drama or glamour. I persuaded him to enter the Diplomatic Service because he was bilingual in French, and he duly entered the year after me, though he had been born the year before. During the war he was with the Free French, and with General Konig throughout the savage battle for Bir Hakeim, until on a sortie to seek help for the beleaguered garrison he was captured when he somehow managed to run into Rommel personally. Later he escaped from his prisoner of war camp in Italy with Hugh Cudlipp and Pat Gibson. He had a talent for concealing great strengths beneath what might strike some as a quiet exterior. He ended up as British Ambassador in Paris.

When we were undergraduates, I spent quite a lot of time with Eddie in Paris, and enjoyed it because he knew the local scene as I did not. We did very ordinary things together and they were fun because they were ordinary. We played third class rugger at Rueil, with railwaymen who cheated; we visited his family and behaved well; drank awful things, and went with ghastly hangovers to the lower grades of racing. I was faintly, and, as usual, incoherently in love with his sister Kiki.

Eddie was often unfluent to the point of being incoherent, but went on patiently, even if everyone got impatient or bored, until he had got his point over. Eddie could also lose friends, for he was quite lazy and his character was never to display *trop de zele*, which means he did remarkably little to keep friendships in repair, and they can just drift away as mine with Nicko Henderson nearly did, after being very close to him in Ernie Bevin's Private Office. It is however, one of Eddie's great strengths that when, sometimes after many years, one does catch up with him, he is exactly the same as when one last saw him.

Eddie shared the ability with Noel Annan of remaining the same and of never acquiring frills or affectations. He was always completely loyal and thought well of one whatever happened without obviously noticing anything had happened.

I remember perhaps the only thing Eddie ever told me which smacked of drama. It was how much, between 1967 and 1969, he had to support, calm, and very often guide Pat Dean after Pat became Ambassador in Washington and seemed more or less to have lost his way and his ability to cope. Involved with MI5, and tipped for the top, Pat had been sent to the United Nations to acquire some overseas experience. He had, however, been an outspoken supporter of Suez, and so when Wilson became Prime Minister in 1964, Pat was moved to Washington where he had less influence. He never recovered from the setback. Eddie's account was so matter-of-fact that one could never have regarded it as disloyalty, and it was indeed not disloyal; just Eddie recording a sad fact.

John Cairncross was also known to me at Trinity. He was somehow persuaded to come from Glasgow to take the Foreign Office exam. It amazed me later when I became Head of Personnel to find, when he was unmasked as a spy, how quickly he had been found to be useless and was bundled off out of harm's way to the Treasury, as the Foreign Office is usually slow and patient in these ways. He was literally useless.

I also knew as undergraduates the men who subsequently became infamous as the spies: Burgess, Philby and, slightly, Maclean. They were all nearly my contemporaries. Of all the future traitors, Guy Burgess was my closest acquaintance: he came to my parties and tried to recruit me to the communist party. I did not like him very much, but he was very interesting: a fascinating shit. An unusually good conversationalist, he was also a well-known practising homosexual at a time when such activities were still illegal. Burgess was brilliantly clever, but not in any applied sense. His practical knowledge was confined to prurience, and he knew every dirty story about everybody. Unpleasant, totally unreliable, and often drunk, he always appeared dirty and unkempt. Perhaps for this reason he made his greatest impression on undergraduates with Labour sympathies. They tended to come from innocent backgrounds and to them Burgess was dazzling.

He particularly appealed to intellectuals. Anthony Blunt, for one, fell in love with him. Steven Runciman said it was widely known at the time. Blunt therefore became a spy as much out of love for Guy Burgess as out of any adherence to Soviet communism, which I thought he must have found particularly revolting to his sensibilities. I was always most surprised at Blunt, out of all the traitors, since I would have thought he would find it too odious having to deal with such people as Russians and communists.

For his part, Kim Philby was clearly thoroughly unprincipled, and fortunately rarely in my company, though I came across him rather dramatically in Amman in December 1962 when he was just about to defect. Donald Maclean was less ostentatious than either in most respects. I followed him into the Foreign Office, and occasionally came across him. When I joined the Personnel department I heard the whisper that he was about to be arrested for his spying only to find he had defected on the next train to Moscow.

There were other friends such as Habby – named after a master at Stowe – whose parents were nice but "common", and he was in constant terror because he was always found out telling big and untrue stories, promising rides in Rolls Royces and then failing to deliver. But I loved him. He was killed in the war too. And Nicko Loftus, who was killed after the war in a motor accident leaving a young family, was a very kind and comforting friend and I still miss him badly.

By far my best friend at Cambridge was Ian Blacker though, whom I really loved. A Harrow mathematician, not especially clever but very musical. The son of a crumbly old house on the Curragh, his family once won the Grand National and hoped – against all the odds – to do so again. He rode well over the hairiest of fences but was not, unlike his peers, half a horse. He had a strong intellectual side – loved music and I remember being flattered to read in his diaries "John Henniker taught me today what real friendship is". He always pretended to complete indifference about the war, but enlisted as soon as he could in my regiment in Italy. His platoon was overrun for the second time by a German attack and he was killed. I lost a lot of friends during the war but his was the greatest loss, the greatest loss of my life perhaps.

THREE

Germany, 1936

My years at Cambridge no doubt affected me and changed my life in several ways. One episode in particular had very profound consequences. Modern languages had been my best subject at Stowe, and I read them at Cambridge, so in the winter of 1933-1934, I visited Germany and France. Hitherto I had learned languages from the equivalent of a Prussian drill sergeant, more or less by rote, but once on the continent I felt my brain really working, perhaps for the first time. My experiences in Germany, in particular, provoked more than simply an intellectual awakening.

I was very much imbued with a horror of what I found. At Cambridge I had learnt about the rise of Hitler, and the suspension of civil society. Once there, it became much more vivid. One never felt safe, and with German friends, we seemed to spend all our time dodging Nazis. The cultural significance of the movement was clearly of the greatest importance. Aryan mythology made me shudder, and does to this day. Of the great ideologies of the age, I regarded German Fascism as much worse than Soviet communism, and so did most of my contemporaries. We had plenty of Bolsheviks at Cambridge, but they were harmless; Nazism was far nastier.

I went to Germany at the right stage of my life, and knew a lot about the language and the country. I stayed in Munich, with Fraurat Krafft, my German teacher. Frau Krafft herself thought the Nazis were unspeakable. One of her daughters was very pro-Nazi, but the other was deeply opposed to them, and there were many furious debates over the dinner table. I found myself very much on the side of my hostess and her cook, a formidable wiry old bird with a rolling pin, which she used on Nazi canvassers.

On the streets swagger sticks were everywhere, and this pseudo-militaristic element in German society I found unbearable. I have always had a visceral reaction against military and semi-military culture, and it was born in Germany. I was disgusted at the involvement of the young and the disadvantaged in frightening the more comfortable middle classes. Rent-a-crowds of young unemployed men were pledged to support Hitler by terrifying his opponents.

The most striking characteristic was the roughness and almost hooliganism of the SA – the Brownshirts. They were always getting drunk and would start butting and bullying people. The Brownshirts were a rabble, the remnants of those found unsuitable for the army. While I was there Ernst Rohm, architect of the SA, had lost a battle with the army for Hitler's affections, was accused of preparing a putsch, and executed. It was a great topic of conversation, and everywhere we heard of sexual impropriety, with the result that Hitler presented himself as the guardian of German morals. The Rohm witch-hunt had a similar, though less dramatic, effect on me as the Bukharin show trial had on Fitzroy Maclean a few years later.

In Nazi Germany it was clear to me that I was in the presence of evil. Following from the general self-deception that Germany had been cheated in the Treaty of Versailles, Hitler turned the invention to his own advantage. Many of the German students with whom I socialised had been involved in the Germanic pure race movements, and felt a great deal of sympathy with Hitler's thesis that Germany had been stabbed in the back by Britain, France and America. By the time I arrived, however, they had come to the conclusion they had been taken for a ride and had backed the wrong horse. Of course, at that point they were already in the saddle, and could not get off.

What I found so amazing, and still do, was why the German people did not stand up to the Nazis, and to their brutalisation. There was constant tension between the Brownshirts and ordinary people. What I found most loathsome about the Nazis was their very easy resort to force. Violence had become acceptable, and it was through that that Germany became what it did a few years later. The streets became violent, and anti-semitism was very obvious even then. Julius Streicher seemed to be everywhere, and was a large and very nasty part of the party. Despite the appeal of Oswald

Mosley, I hoped that similar developments would not have happened in Britain, though I rather thought they might, and I saw a little of it later in the East End of London.

I personally saw Hitler several times. What was striking was that he was so ordinary: a mouldy looking fellow, in a seedy raincoat, always saluting. I thought him filthy and his militaristic affectations disgusting. He was second-rate in every respect: a man of little intellect, and less presence. On the occasions I heard him give speeches, he was clearly an effective orator, albeit one of pure hatred. His talent was as a drummer, and to his rhythm Germans marched. His success has never satisfactorily been explained to me; it is a matter I still explore.

While I was in Germany I visited Yugoslavia for the first time, little knowing the significance the country would have in my future. Ian Blacker who had been selected to be Honorary Attaché in Athens, called me, and offered to take me to Yugoslavia on his way there. Foolishly, and inadvertently, Ian and I left Munich on the day of Hitler's first meeting with Mussolini. We thus attracted the attention of a swarm of blackcoated policemen. There seemed to be one behind every tree.

We proceeded slowly along often flooded roads towards Mostar. Since we were in a foreign car, we were greeted with a great fanfare. The Yugoslavs had been expecting the Czech Foreign Minister. Ian and I went on to Dubrovnik, where we parted and embarked in different directions; I had a German with me, and we went off to Venice, and thence back to Munich. With Ian, I had done no more than get a faint, but fascinating and tempting whiff of Yugoslavia. It was a lovely country, and I recall how attractive the mixed communities in Sarajevo were. For the sum of one shilling I spent a night at Jajce, a charming town of mosques with a splendid waterfall. Dubrovnick was to me the most beautiful city I had ever seen and remains so. Bosnia was lovely, wild, and underneath a little sinister. There was everywhere very much a sense of the meeting of East and West.

I returned home from Germany, absolutely convinced there would be war. The Germans were playing soldiers, and I certainly expected war. I thought that only through war would the evil I had seen be destroyed. It remained to be seen whether we would stand up to the threat. Some of my friends also went to Germany at around this time, though it did not seem to have had the same effect on them. It affected me so strongly probably because I went on my own. The trip changed my life in two ways. Firstly my choice of career, or at least of ambition, had been decided: I had originally wanted to be a doctor; after visiting Germany I wanted to join the Foreign Office as a diplomat. Secondly, by 1935, I was firmly of the opinion that if there was to be a war, I must be in it.

FOUR

The Foreign Office, 1938 to 1940

The trip was greatly beneficial, and I managed to get a first in my German paper back at Cambridge. By the time I graduated I was a very different person to the callow youth who went up three years earlier. While there I had made many friends, and taken the key decision that would affect the rest of my life. I loved my time there. Cambridge ended with us all becoming 21 simultaneously. We all had twenty-first birthday parties, and I fell in love with various people. Since I did not have any money, I never considered that things would ever go very far, and certainly not to marriage. I was not terribly precocious. Promiscuity was not at all common then and certainly not as far as I was concerned.

Deciding to go into the Foreign Office was one thing; being accepted was another. The Foreign Office had a very great reputation, the greatest in Whitehall, and I was not sure if I would be good enough to get in. To attempt to redress this I went to a school to learn how to be a diplomat. Next to the British Museum, one Monsieur Mangeot ran a cramming college for those of us planning to apply to the Foreign Office. Further education of this kind was required for we needed to know subjects which were not part of any degree course. A little elementary economics, several subjects in early modern history, international law, in which I was quite good, and political theory, the study of which convinced me that I was not an intellectual: I was terrible at it from the start, and I remained terrible.

I went back to Germany to brush up on my German, and had my earlier opinions confirmed. For her part Fraurat Krafft was resigned to the course of events. From Germany I visited France, and went to stay with Monsieur

Martin, my *ancien professeur*, through whose hands Terence Rattigan had passed the year before, and who turned the experience into a very funny fable, *French Without Tears*. Terence had been thrown out of Harrow after I had seem him at Lords and had become a much more dissolute character.

Martin met my train at La Gare du Nord: an extraordinary figure in black, with a huge beard. I stayed with him at his house, with his tyrant wife and his daughter who had attracted Rattigan's attention, and had mischievously been portrayed by him as a figure of great glamour. She was in fact not a bit glamorous, was quite skinny, and was usually in the company of her boyfriend, a Basque dwarf. I had an amusing time there, meeting Martin's curious friends, and playing tennis with both Jardine, a very clever man, and Scot Fox, a very conceited man, both of whom were also cramming for the Foreign Office. Monsieur Martin ruled with a rod of iron, and labelled me *le garçon travailleur*.

Application was no bad thing. Of all Civil Service examinations, that of the Foreign Office was the longest of all. I went to London for the Foreign Office exams on the cheap, though my journey had a hidden cost. I hitched a ride from Cambridge to London on the back of Collins Lewis's motorcycle "The Flying Fornicator". Collins was a Welshman who had been with me at Stowe, and remained a friend at Cambridge. He was notable for the huge black mackintosh he wore which enabled him to travel through bad weather. We arrived, and I bade him goodbye. The next day I heard that he had been killed on the way back to Cambridge. Fortunately, for my conscience at any rate, he had been going to London anyway.

The year before me, Jardine passed top in the examination, but he was taken to a medical at the Civil Service Commission and it was discovered that he could not go to one place in the world, La Paz, Bolivia, and so he was ruled out. It was amazingly unfair, but a Foreign Office rule. He was, however, allowed in years later, but was always regarded as being of dubious health, and never really became established. Most of those who sat the exam with me were unsuccessful, and many then went elsewhere.

It was for me a great surprise to pass into the Foreign Office. Even my kindest supporters saw me as a very long priced outsider and I could not believe it when suddenly one day when I was out shooting with my uncle my mother came staggering through the sugar beet waving a telegram. I came top in the exam and joined the Foreign Office a month or so later. I did not however come top in the year: Francis Brown beat me in the interview. I was, nevertheless, the first boy from Stowe to enter the Service, something of which I was very proud. Public school was, moreover a perfectly good preparation. Though people were increasingly coming in from outside to join the Foreign Service, it remained a public school preserve.

On my first day I walked straight into the Foreign Office building in Whitehall, to be met by the Assistant Private Secretary to the Secretary of State, Derick Hoyer-Millar, who was in charge of Personnel. I went to a room with other new recruits. We were addressed by Hoyer-Millar. "Congratulations on passing," he said. "Where would you all like to go?" As we stood around, it became clear that everybody knew exactly where they wanted to go except for me. My first posting was not something to which I had given much thought: I had not expected to get into the Foreign Office at all, and indeed my success had been a great surprise to me. My assumption was that most of the new men would ask for Washington or Paris, so I asked for Tokyo. "You can't go there for your first posting," was the incredulous response.

Probably as a result of my request, I was placed in the Far Eastern department. The Foreign Office tries to accede to wishes, and the post preference card was a convention to which I attached great importance when my time came to run Personnel. Bob Howe was the Head of the Far Eastern department when I joined. He was the top example of the Diplomatic Service, the model to which we aspired. A beneficiary of open competition, recently introduced into the Service, Howe was the son of an engine driver, and was the first of his ilk to get as high as he did. Bob had been wounded in Shanghai when the Japanese machine-gunned his car. He was a very nice man, who eventually became Governor General of Sudan. The second-in-command was Ashley Clarke, who later became Chief Clerk and Ambassador in Rome. It was a good career, and Clarke taught me a great deal. Once he was given Rome he stuck to it like limpet. When I was Head of Personnel I knew it was my job to try and get him out. He remained there for nine years.

I was in effect assistant to Bill Denning who had recently returned from Japan, and later became Ambassador in Tokyo. He had been with Mountbatten whom he absolutely hated.

The man who was responsible for me was Nigel Ronald, a former

Guardsman who had been badly wounded in the First World War. A very clever man, he went to extraordinary pains to teach me how to be a clerk, and I was always enormously grateful. I would write page after page of dictation, which he assiduously checked. "You have to be accurate, my boy." There were always three or four of us in the room so being taught, or, rather, learning; the Foreign Office never really teaches any of its recruits. When my turn came to write a paper, if at the end of it the word "the" remained, I had done all right; everything else had been crossed out.

On my first day in the Far Eastern department I was given some intelligence about cabotage in the Dutch East Indies. I remember copying very long minutes from the Legal department concerning a subject I knew absolutely nothing about. Generally, we wrote minutes, received intelligence, saw people, and tried to find out what was happening. I found the work very interesting, and far less abstruse than I expected. We were given our head to a great extent, and many decisions rested with us, not the least being the question of whether to pass a matter up to a higher Secretary as being of sufficient importance.

There was quite a lot going on in the region, mostly intrigues on the part of the Japanese. Through our trading interests and the role of Hong Kong, they were generally of some importance. Soon after I arrived, a ship arrived in London and blew up, and we blamed the Japanese, prompting a tremendous row. Timor was a subject of mine, for it aroused Japanese appetites; our concern was the presence of Japanese stooges and frontmen on the island. I was responsible for the Burma Road, which we were trying to build. There were concerns over Tibet, and our mission in Nepal, over which we dealt with the India Office, neither party knowing for certain in whose remit Nepal lay. I had also to deal with the Siamese, who were proposing a non-aggression pact to safeguard us both from the Japanese. I thought it was an absolutely wizard idea, and sent it up to Sir Alex Cadogan, the Permanent Secretary. I was very pleased that permission was granted for me to take it further, and the agreement was eventually signed by our man in Siam, Sir Joshua Crosby, a very stuffy old bird. I did not think it did anybody any good at all, however. It was about worth the paper it was written on, if that.

As impressive as the Foreign Office building was, once inside, comparative informality prevailed. I once called a tremendously grand and austere superior "Sir". "Sir? You're never to use that word again," he snapped. There were curious gatherings in the Third Room, or the mess, where we all had tea together. Inside there were all sorts of oddities who had somehow crept into corners of the Foreign Office and were made Sir George Somebody, or Sir Alexander Someone; no one knew what the hell they had done, or what they were doing. They had come up through various administrative departments, were given a gong, and were probably retained to add a bit of wisdom at tea-time.

The Foreign Office was not quite so rigorous then as it was later to become. At the time I joined it was coming to the end of an era in which men could spend their entire careers there and never leave London. As a junior with a yearning to learn something about anything, I was itching to go abroad. Others fell by the wayside. We had, for instance, the Prize Poodles: men who had been at Eton or Winchester and who had passed every test and examination with flying colours, but who thereafter slowed down and eventually burnt out. Their rosettes proved to be tarnished, and they became a great disappointment, most of all to themselves. John Cairncross was one; Dick Heppel another. There are intellectuals and there are doers; I am certainly in the latter category. One needs to be quick in the Foreign Office. There were of course some people who were neither intellectuals nor doers, as Harold Nicholson later divulged.

For a third class clerk, there was little outside the Foreign Office building. Our contact with politicians was minimal. My only exposure to them occurred when I used to go for walks around St James's Park with Rab Butler, who sought information, material for speeches, and continually boasted about what he was doing in the House of Commons stressing his horror at the outrages committed by the Japanese. Terence Rattigan did not need to boast. Terence had been in France before me, and had established a reputation for being fast and loose. He was homosexual, but not exclusively so, and radiated the qualities of a very successful public schoolboy. He had been in the Harrow XI against Eton, and I watched him when I was at Broadstairs. The year after he was thrown out and became a more dissolute character, and a playwright. Though I never saw him with his trousers round his ankles, rumours of Terence's multifarious assignations in the Secretary of State's room were legion.

While I was concerned with belligerent overtures in the Far East, the threat of war closer to home was palpable. My fears of five years earlier were being realised. Though the policy of the government was to try and reach an accommodation with Hitler, there were voices warning as to the danger – such as those of Vansittart and Winston – but they were mainly in the undergrowth. We did not know at the time that, though he had his faults, Winston usually came up with the right answer. Chamberlain's government was hoping to get through the difficult time with Hitler, reach the other side into clearish water, and hope for the best. It was almost impossible to discuss openly that which concerned us most – whether war would come – because we thought that one false step might make it more likely.

It was quite clear it was Chamberlain's policy, and since no one in government repudiated it, it was accepted. The Foreign Office, however, did not believe in the policy. My own feeling was very anti-appeasement, as was that of my generation as I knew them. I had entered the Foreign Office with Ralph Selby, who was the son of our Ambassador in Vienna. He had been through the Anschluss in March 1938, and was horrified about what the Germans had done. He had gone to rallies organised by *Kraft durch Freude*, found them the most insidious things he had ever seen: Germans sitting out in the sun, getting beautifully brown, singing songs, and drinking beer. I visited him when his father was Ambassador in Lisbon, and his description of the growing confidence of Germans was a great influence on me. Sir Walford Selby had been left with a sad feeling that he had not played his proper part in the earlier war. He added breadth and depth to my own feelings about Germany. On the most germane matter I remained convinced: there would be a war, and I had to fight in it.

I was watching with Ralph Selby from the Foreign Office when Chamberlain arrived in Downing Street after returning from Munich. We saw him wave his piece of paper, and we were hopping mad. There was nothing we could do. A generation older than me, Con O'Neill resigned publicly, and many of us were glad when he was taken back into the Foreign Office. I had the highest regard for Con; he always made me feel that there was a heart in the Foreign Office alongside a brain.

Resignations were rare, though the sentiment was common. In a way the vast Foreign Office building was looking down morally as well as physically on Downing Street. Chamberlain did not act on the advice of the Foreign Office, but of the Tory party; backbench and frontbench. The country too, it has to be said, were desperate to avoid war. I think it would have been quite acceptable if Chamberlain had gone to Munich carrying a bit of paper, already having commanded the maximum rearmament of Britain, and gone to make what peace he could with Hitler. Everybody would have applauded that; we knew we had to re-arm as fast as we could. I think our feeling of betrayal was that Chamberlain, though he did re-arm, in no way did so wholeheartedly. As it was, we sent Neville Henderson to be our Ambassador in Berlin because he got on with Goering. They went off shooting together, great friends. I was equally appalled at the implications of Edward VIII's treachery when he too went off to see Hitler.

We heard how conditions on the continent deteriorated, and war seemed inevitable. Sir Eric Phipps, who as Ambassador went in 1937 from Berlin to Paris, saw events better than most. His daughter came to stay with me in Suffolk recently and said she found the French very *poule* – scared. We hoped that the French would be strong and that the army would be powerful. But things were different. Everyone who returned from France confirmed our fears.

When I started to work in the Office, it was exciting to leave for London with a recommendation that I should stay with a friend of a neighbour. I had scarcely moved in when the war started and I had to decline a most tempting invitation from two girls I had recently met at a dance to go to Scotland. After some months we were fitted out by our tailors with the appropriate uniform to attend a levée and thought we looked marvellous. But standing alongside a new second lieutenant from one of the smarter Scottish regiments revealed how dull we looked.

I realised very quickly that I could hardly afford to live in London on my pay, which at that time was £300 a year, and I soon began to look for an alternative place to live. I talked to my friends who had passed into the Service with me and heard that the Foreign Office were prepared to accommodate and provide a man to cook for up to three young secretaries to sit upstairs and deal with any urgent communication that came in the night. I applied and was lucky enough to get a place. It was marvellous training. By day I worked in the Far Eastern department struggling with my particular assignment, and by night the whole world would deluge the resident clerk with information.

The resident clerks' room was a hive of activity at night. It was a meeting place for those in the office who wanted excitement and were involved in the talk of war. Amongst those wandering in were Terence Rattigan and Fitzroy Maclean. Maclean had come back bored from Moscow and prowled around the Northern department looking for trouble and not exactly excited that his clients were mainly Icelanders complaining about fish. It was a meeting which held future promise for me after we had made real friends on a trip to see Berkeley Gage and his German wife – whose marriage didn't last long once the war was underway.

There were other excitements. I had been put – when I entered the Service – in the cipher room where a lot of old soldiers from the First World War had found a billet. They spent each day repeating long columns of numbers, which they then deciphered. I was rather happy there. I shared a room with a very nice man who was enormously helpful. He seemed – cleverly – to know that I was overworked, and when the time came for us to go home he always kindly offered to put my papers away. Being naturally afraid of keys and ciphers getting muddled, I keenly accepted his kindness. It was only later when the police called to speak to him that I learnt he was a spy. He went down for something like 15 years. I think his name was Joe King. A very nice man, I thought. He was spying for the Russians.

One evening, the Embassy in Berlin rang the resident clerks and Adrian Holman gave us the following message: "Same man, same time, same place". I was baffled. Philip immediately said he must be coming by air so we had to ring the air ministry and found through their resident clerk that they knew all about it. It was an emissary, Dr. Dibelius, a Swede who had been sent by Goering to try and persuade us not to declare war on Germany. Mussolini was also trying to forestall our belligerency. It amounted to nothing. We knew of the declaration of war before Chamberlain gave his broadcast. We heard it in the Foreign Office. I had hoped it was coming, but was afraid it would not.

One night the Embassy in Oslo rang up. "There's a ship steaming up the fjord," the Ambassador said. "Now it's opened fire." The Germans had started the invasion. One of our chaps in Narvik later said that it was very nasty, and that no battle was made to be fought in a fjord: one shoots and simply cannot miss. I was also the first person to hear of the invasion of Albania. Over the telephone we also heard of the Sudetenland, and Czechoslovakia; then Poland. One night a grouchy Winston rang up, as he was increasingly to do. He wanted to know what Hitler had said to the Ambassador. I said "I can't tell you sir, you are not in the Cabinet". Winston growled.

Though I was relieved that we had finally issued the declaration, life was very exciting once the war began. The work was ceaseless. I operated in the Far Eastern department in the day, and was duty officer all night. All of us had to decipher all telegrams ourselves. One of them was Mussolini's declaration of war. Such messages presented problems, since the Secretary of State, Halifax, had given strict orders not to wake him at night.

FIVE

Going to war, 1941 and 1942

Oddly enough, joining the army in the middle of a war was not easy. The Foreign Office was extremely reluctant to accede to my request, as they had been with Fitzroy's. Ours was a reserved occupation. Threats were made that in the event of my enlisting, my career in diplomacy was forfeit. The Service was not keen on its staff wandering off to fight. Lees-Mayall, whose best man I had been in a wedding of which we all disapproved, had left the Foreign Office in uniform, only to be brought back and deposited in Whitehall. Soon after, he and his unfortunate wife were sent off to Berne, where they spent the war in considerable misery. It was a salutary lesson, and not just for me, so I waited rather than running off to enlist.

I went at various intervals to the War Office, for interviews. On one occasion I found myself in a large room full of long-haired men. I had sat there for a long time, feeling rather puzzled, until someone turned to me and asked: "What's your objection mate?" I said, "I don't have any objection. I don't want to object". This attracted astonished glances; I was in the wrong place. They were all conscientious objectors.

I continued to apply, and finally the War Office told me that the regulations for junior diplomats had been relaxed and that the Foreign Office could no longer prevent my being called up. I went in to see Ivo Mallet, Private Secretary to the Secretary of State, and said, "I'm off to join the army, unless you disapprove". He said, "I do disapprove. Very much. You oughtn't to do that. But we shall tell the Secretary of State, who will no doubt be very angry with you, and tell you that there won't be a place for you after the war". A week later I went in to see the Secretary of State, Anthony Eden. He was not angry at all. "You had better go if the War Office wants you. We'll try to get you out afterwards. Give my love to Strafer Gott," a Rifle Brigade General in North Africa, later to be killed in an air crash when he was about to take command in the Middle East.

So it was that I was enlisted in the Essex Regiment from which I got a Regular Army Emergency Commission as a Second Lieutenant in the Rifle Brigade on 15th March 1941. I went off with the Essex to Blandford, Dorset, where I received my first training, and joined a coastal defence battalion. I suspect too many people were being called up and we had to be kept occupied. At one point we went on to an island, where we were armed with rattles rather than guns. I doubt that we would have proved a great obstacle in the event of an invasion. We dug a large trench to fortify Blandford against German attack which eventually turned out to be facing the wrong way so we filled it in again.

When the immediate danger of invasion passed, I was sent off in the Essex Regiment to Brentwood. When my East End companions there were sent off to the Near East to fight the Italians, I felt rather guilty to be sent for officer training on the Isle of Man. It was quite interesting to go to Government House for dinner, where my grandfather had been Governor. Otherwise it was cold and windy, and I occupied myself by captaining the rugby team. At the end of the training I passed out.

I had asked for a transfer from the Essex Regiment in order to join the Rifle Brigade, in which my Uncle Charlie had, in the First World War, commanded the Third Battalion. Based at Winchester, the regiment was culturally and geographically a good deal more heterogeneous than my previous one. A lightly armed infantry regiment, formed by Sir John Moore in the Peninsula War, our primary role in war was speedy advance. We were intended to be small men marching 90 paces to the minute.

Most of the other ranks in the Rifle Brigade came from the East End of London and were by definition severely deprived of many of the better things in life. Some were in every way hopeless but when they were good they could be very good. I managed to get two appointed corporals, which gave them some authority. One a real working class boy from a difficult home in London turned out to be absolutely first class, but both did well and both were good to work with. It was interesting seeing how young men brought up in conditions which could only be called very poor somehow adapted themselves to new circumstances. They had a natural habit of noticing everything that went on around them – often one could not hope that they would be able to read a map but to tell them to go and find water in the desert, was well within their compass. They would steal some or find some and when they came to retrace their steps they would have noticed quite small things that acted as markers and knew where they were.

Later on in the desert, I had great difficulty with a soldier who refused to obey orders and would not get out of bed. I told my sergeant that if he refused to move, he was to beat him up and put him on a charge for disobedience. When I got back this had been done. As we left camp we ran into a German unit. The rifleman on the truck came to and got very angry. He asked to be given a grenade and when we gave it to him, he ran off to a German tank. He dropped it down the hatch and blew the tank up. After too much strain courage gives way and one becomes totally lacking in that quality, only for it to be revived by a crisis. It was useful to understand these things.

I joined the Rifle Brigade at Tidworth where I was then put on a draft to the Middle East at my own urgent request. Before long I was climbing on a troopship in Glasgow, and we were off to the Middle East, via the Cape. A very long voyage, necessary because we had no naval capability in the Mediterranean. We lost one man before we arrived in Freetown harbour in a drunken brawl.

I met my battalion at Girawla, on the Mediterranean coast of Egypt. I was put into "B" Company, where I was quickly trained for desert warfare under Hugo Garmoyle. One of the first things to be learnt about desert warfare is that one never knows where the hell one is. Redressing this involved being sent off into the desert in a truck with an armoured car in attendance, but otherwise quite alone. There was no means of navigation except for a compass, which I had never really used before. We went off for a day or two into Libya, avoiding Italians, and then headed back. My skills as a navigator were put to a real test. In the middle of a great desert, I thought I would never find my battalion. The last building we had seen was Fort Madelena. I drove on, getting depressed. Then, suddenly, as I went over a sand hill, I looked down and was amazed to see the battalion below.

This navigation episode gave me enormous confidence, which was

Kit Nicholl, Ian Blacker and J.H. at Sandhurst

essential in that theatre of war. Contrary to expectations, the desert is not at all an unpleasant place in which to fight. It is, in fact, very pleasant: dry, healthy, fresh, no smells. There were not many flies where I was, and the heat was easily bearable. There were no civilians, no secret service or SS; just army against army, and Rommel seemed a decent and honourable enemy. I was certainly happier to be there than on a North Atlantic convoy.

The use of comparatively small armoured units meant that war in the desert, with few natural barriers, was quite fluid. Fronts could swiftly be formed in any direction, and the risks of being outflanked lessened accordingly. My battalion was part of the Seventh Armoured Division, the Desert Rats. One day we were about to engage the Germans, who had recently arrived near us. We went off to find them, three or four armoured brigades, in columns. We first probed the Italians on the flank. A little later we met Germans in the battle of Sidi Rezegh. This "fierce clash" as Churchill later described it, took place in November 1942, and was the opening of General Auchinlecks's offensive, the ultimate objective of which was the relief of Tobruk. My predominant reaction was, "Thank God I'm here, let's get on with it." I was itching to go, and glad to have made it before the war was over.

The North African campaign came to a virtual halt after the British victories in Libya which almost eliminated any activity by the Italians whose strength in trained fighting men was very low. The British brought up and strengthened the line to the Egyptian frontier, and had, in the fighting, extended it to Tobruk. The land up to the Egyptian frontier was occupied by troops from Egypt and new faces brought over from Britain. These moved forward to strengthen the forces in Tobruk and westwards.

British columns moved eastwards from the forces we had in Libya, and our battalion pushed forward to the frontiers of Libya and did a little patrolling towards the east. It was there that crushing British victories at Bengazhi and Sidi Barrani immobilised the Italian armies in North Africa. My battalion ended up keeping a watch on the western end of the British forces in North Africa and we occupied from time to time Forts Mecheli, Msus, and Derna to prevent any move by the Germans and Italians re-starting their offensive in North Africa. It was from this line that our battalion was recalled to Cairo for re-equipping and refitting against a need to increase pressure on the Italians in Libya and Tripoli. To forestall this, the Germans began to send troops in increasing numbers to underpin the Italians. This did not at the early stage appear to endanger the British position, but gradually the German effort increased and with it a further strengthening of Italian forces.

As my battalion prepared to withdraw for refit in Cairo we were warned that if there were a scare about further enemy thrusts to the east, our return to Cairo would be halted by the sending of a codeword. We were delighted to receive no such word and proceeded on to Cairo for our rest and refit and a good deal of enjoyment. We passed through our troops on the Western Front where a small offensive led by heavy tanks had made some progress with a few casualties. Alertness was important on this exposed front. The strength of our troops on this front was marginally reduced by the withdrawal of a few men under Quintin Hogg, later Lord Hailsham, from our own lines. Otherwise troops like the two or three companies from one battalion which were serving in the area were kept up to strength and continued regularly to send out patrols to warn us of any movement forward by the enemy.

We continued with our training steadily both in that area and in Egypt itself. At the end of our refitting period troops were moved back to the frontier area and were given new weapons as we began to prepare for a new offensive westwards to eliminate the Italians there. Simultaneously the arrival of German troops in Libya in increasing numbers was becoming apparent and we started sending out more patrols westwards to ensure that we were not surprised.

The line running south from Gaza was itself strengthened and it was felt for the time being that would be enough to withstand any threat to Tobruk. The company, with which I was now serving, had moved to the western end of our line and we were engaged in one or two more adventurous patrols. Throughout the next month or two patrolling became more and more active. There was concern that new troops under Rommel's command constituted a more immediate threat and our troops were therefore strengthened by reinforcements from Cairo. More British and South African armoured cars increased our strength and a series of "boxes" were created southwards near Gazala to bar any further enemy advances.

As summer started, there was more and more talk of attack in what was called "Rommel weather", which kept us on our toes patrolling in murky sandstorms. There was also talk of many more troops landing and preparing for a German offensive. My battalion began to dig a box to interrupt any march from the east and supported a box formed by Indian troops from the south. We all knew we had to work fast to be ready in time. Suddenly messages began to come in from the South African armoured cars on our southern flank; the Germans were on the move, and our box was quickly overrun by them. They passed through in sight of most of us in columns – all armed with shovels over their shoulders for digging – towards a new headquarters nearer the sea and Tobruk. There was a new offensive on the Free French forces in Bir Hakeim where General Konig had ordered his troops to stand and fight and were regularly bombed two or three times a day by the German airforce. Tom Bird was ordered to take a company to help and encourage the French in their resistance, and my company was ordered to lie close up to help them if needed.

News began to accumulate of more and more successful attacks by the Germans on the centre of the Gazala line which we had hitherto thought was relatively safe and in one of which my brother Dick was captured with some of the artillery of the Tyne and Tees Division. Dick had gone off to do some spotting, but was captured, and taken to Padua in Italy. In his prisoner of war camp he bumped into Eddie Tomkins. When the Germans moved out of Italy, they took all the prisoners with them to Germany, and he spent the rest of the war in PoW camps. Dick was fortunately much too big to fit in a tunnel, and so was omitted from escape parties.

The fighting was even fiercer near Tobruk, towards which the German offensive was clearly aimed. Having been outflanked by the Germans the troops in our battalion moved towards the coast and we joined the battle for Tobruk in the area of Sidi Rezegh. All the troops in our area were engaged in the battle of Knightsbridge and our battalion, after probing the Italians, were fully involved in the battle. It was my first serious engagement in the war and it was exhilarating to be there after all the efforts I had made to get into the war.

We went through the Germans on the Capuzzo Track. My colonel went up and down the line, ensuring all the vehicles were in place. Our job was to protect the guns from the German infantry at Sidi Rezegh aerodrome. German guns had much longer range than ours, and we could not get near enough to do any damage. After skirmishing throughout the day, my company came up late at night towards the airfield. The Germans started firing at us, and my Company commander, Jimmy McGregor, was killed in front of me. We withdrew to the other side of the valley and dug in for the night. Early next morning we were woken up by fearful banging and shouting: a line of German tanks were moving along the ridge we were on. One must remember it was my first battle. I had no idea what to do. My sergeant rushed up to me. "For Christ's sake get out of it". "Oh, no," I said, "we must stand and fight." He strongly disagreed, and since his opinion was a lot more firmly held than mine, and since we could not in any case do much against tanks, I climbed on board a truck, and we withdrew hastily from the battle.

The Germans withdrew to the airfield, and we withdrew to the south without sustaining any casualties. I was very pleased with the sergeant who had rescued me from ridiculous folly. We went off at night towards Cairo, when our commander, General Cunningham, seemed very uncertain and bewildered by the speed of the German advance. As we moved along we saw a column of armour on our right. Someone claimed that it was the Fourth Armoured Brigade. I ventured to doubt it. It did not in the least look like the Fourth Armoured Brigade. I decided to go up to the front to tell them it was not the Fourth Armoured Brigade. As I returned hairy fellows on a motorbike and sidecar came up to us and the commander fired a Very pistol into the air. All hell was let loose. They were wearing the feathered hat of the Bersaglieri. It was an Italian column from the west.

We had been told that if anything went wrong in the night, we were to head immediately for Cairo, or the Siwa oasis. A lot of people whizzed off in various directions. I decided not to, since my truck was stuck in the sand. Everyone else got out and ran off, and eventually I extricated myself. Those of us who were left went off north towards Sidi Barani and we got together with the remainder of our force. Throughout the rest of the night as we moved back we could hear the Italian wireless jabbering away saying that they had got the enemy, then that they had lost him. They had in fact driven through our headquarters and come out the other side without noticing. We all seemed to be in retreat, and nobody knew who had won.

The war went on in this way. We would go off in columns against the Germans with the day's orders, and then come back. We probed each other. My command was 10 Bren gun carriers, fortunately, for our tanks were not always reliable. We had Crusaders for the first time, and we thought they were marvellous tanks. They looked beautiful, but they had an unfortunate defect. When the carburettor got at all hot, the tank stopped. This was problematic in desert warfare. A line of us would suddenly come to a halt, on a ridge.

Fighting is hard to describe to someone fortunate enough not to have experienced it, and battle usually feels more like muddle. I do not think I ever killed anyone in hand to hand combat, and cannot remember killing anyone at all. There was always some distance involved, and I was usually concerned with ensuring our guns were firing unharmed, and ensuring the enemy did not overrun them. War as I experienced had little to do with the close-quarter combat usually depicted in the cinema.

I was wounded one day, at El Adem, near Tobruk. Desmond Prettie, a Major in the Rifle Brigade was standing with his two Honey tanks, which seemed to be under his command, facing the Germans. I agreed with him to move on against the Germans. At the moment I put up my blue flag and the others started following me a Honey tank was hit by a shell, and had to stop. We went on across the front of the German troops with my three carriers and the Bren guns engaging some of them with fire. As my carrier had been knocked out the day before, I had a new driver that day who did not understand my hand signals. We drove on further than I had meant to signal and one of my carriers was hit. Rifleman Featherstone was killed and I turned towards the German gun. I saw a German soldier stand up and clamber up the gun. He fired and hit my carrier throwing a mass of metal into my back at very close range. My carrier NCO, Lance Corporal Newman, said "You'll have to lie down". I said I would not and jumped over the side of the carrier and set off to punish the German gunners, whereupon he chased me and pointed to my back, which was pretty mangled. He put me back in the Bren Carrier. My battalion came up to give covering fire and protect us and several Germans came over and lay down by me. They had surrendered to us. I lay there most of the afternoon. We had been knocked out of the battle. As it got dark we were rescued.

I was taken to the casualty station without loosing consciousness. I looked up to see various figures. I said to one of them "Who are you?" and he replied, "My name's Wilson," a New Zealander. With him was Windsor Lewis, who had been at Cambridge with me. A rugby blue, he had played for Wales. It turned out that I had been shot clean through the lung. They dealt with me, proceeded to sew me up, and then they decided that I was not fit enough to proceed to Cairo for treatment, as my battalion had arranged. I was slung in the back of a truck and taken to Tobruk, to the next dressing station. We then went on to Mersa Matruh, a coastal town near Alexandria. My commanding officer had arranged a plane for me, but I was too ill to fly, so I was taken by ambulance to Cairo, where doctors, Professor Logan from Newcastle Royal Infirmary, and Dr. Nicolson from the Brompton Chest Hospital, looked after me at the number one thoracic hospital in Egypt, the Hospital Heliopolis. Logan was a tough fellow, but an excellent surgeon, and was extremely kind to me. He probably saved my life. He put me in his room so he could keep an eye on me. I was touched that while I was in Cairo, Wilson and Lewis popped in to see how I was. I had been told in the hospital that I had been lucky to get that far, and that I did was due to Wilson and Lewis.

I was told I would recover, and was sent south to convalesce. The wound needed to heal, which it would not do in Cairo, but might in South Africa. A good climate was required, and the Cape would provide it. I went down by ship from Suez. As I got on the troop ship I saw a face through the wire I recognised from a previous encounter in the war. A soldier I knew from Sidi Rezegh. At that time he was bright and promising and a platoon sergeant under Peter Innes, who got an MC in that battle. The soldier I saw had been much commended for his part in getting Peter that decoration but obviously something awful had happened in the meantime, desertion or dereliction of duty of some kind, for he was handcuffed to the wire. I didn't have time to do more than wave at him and wish him good luck, but his face betrayed that there was little chance. I think he was on his way back to Britain for court martial. I have puzzled much ever since about what happened. I came to the conclusion that no one has a monolithic share of courage. The amount of courage one can draw upon every day is limited. If with his record he was thought to have been derelict in his duty, it must have been serious.

South Africa was in a funny state. Most of the doctors had gone to help the troops in the north, and the medical service was at a low ebb, but was sufficient to help me through the last stages of my recovery. Ostensibly everyone was patting one on the back; underneath there was much hostility, and on one occasion in civilian clothes I was given a white feather. But we enjoyed ourselves and were asked out to farms and parties. I occasionally noticed that the black Africans were harshly treated. I asked one farmer "why do they eat different food from us?" He said they prefer their food to ours. I am quite sure it was very much poorer food. It was a cause of discontent, and it was apparent amongst the South Africans with whom I had fought, that the blacks and whites had different diets.

Other than play bridge most of the time, I fell in love briefly with my physiotherapist. She was very beautiful. I was very innocent. There was a chance of picking up a tart, but I did not avail myself of that. That was a part of my education to come. I left with pangs for the two physiotherapists, which were not resolved by kissing them goodbye.

After a year convalescing I began to enquire how I was to get back to the Middle East. I chose a Belgian Congo river steamer. It was great fun. I was the only passenger with two other women, we played bridge with the captain, a medical worker, who could make slams with practically no cards at all. I learnt a rather savage type of bridge. We arrived back in Suez after a short stay in Aden where I had a sinus operation. Marching through the streets of Cairo I was spotted from his flat by Fitzroy Maclean.

My colonel received a call from the Military Secretary for me to report to General Headquarters. I told them that I was anxious to go back to my battalion in Libya. I was told in turn that I had to report to Lieutenant Colonel Purdon to go to battle school in the Canal Zone, in order to get a movement order to get back to the battalion. When I reached Purdon, he said "You are exactly what I want". I said I wanted to go back to my battalion, to which he replied: "You may want to, but you're not going to. I need you here to teach these chaps here about battle. You have been in battle. None of my other officers have." I was very upset, but was promised that I would be replaced when someone else turned up.

With ill grace I settled down, and started playing bridge again.

My trainees were South Africans who were to be forged into an armoured division. I had to take them out into the desert, give them a map reference and let them get on with it. They were not awfully good, which surprised me, because they were big, tough, rugged men. The problem was that they were not very bright. They tended to go straight across country, ignoring their bearing, and looking neither to the right nor to the left, driving over cliffs and down holes. It was a nasty surprise to see them come back covered in blood and with their heads in bandages. Battle school was more dangerous than battle.

Next came our rather futile attempt to simulate battle conditions. We took the trainees out on exercise into the desert in buses with live ammunition. They never seemed quite to understand this, and would discharge whole magazines into the seat in front. One of them was cleaning his gun when he blew his shoulder off; another shot someone else in the leg. I had had quite enough of this, and wrote, increasingly desperately, to my regiment, pleading for them to take me away. Eventually I was called to GHQ Cairo. When I arrived I was told that I was to see Brigadier Fitzroy Maclean. I didn't know he had been made a brigadier. I gathered he seemed to think I might be useful for a secret mission he was organising.

SIX

Yugoslavia, 1943 to 1945

The Military Secretary at British Headquarters told me that Brigadier Maclean wanted me to go with his mission to Yugoslavia. As he later put it, he thought my "combination of military and diplomatic training should be very useful for our kind of job". The Military Secretary was very vague about what the mission might involve, but stipulated that I was only to go as a volunteer. I knew nothing of Yugoslavia except for my trip from Munich with Ian Blacker.

In making my decision there were two principal considerations: family and regimental. My parents had had a bad time with my being wounded before my brother went missing and was later discovered to be a prisoner of war, and I did not gratuitously wish to exacerbate their worry by volunteering to disappear into an unknown and rather problematical part of Europe. I went to Alexandria and saw my commanding officer, Tom Pearson, and presented him with my dilemma. "I am very flattered to have been asked," I said, "but I don't know whether or not to accept." I was attracted because the mission sounded a good deal more exciting than what I had been doing, but I was also alive to the potential dangers. I was to be Tom's Adjutant, and he said he would be sorry to lose me. I was put on a plane for Algiers, to see Lieutenant General Sir Henry Maitland Wilson, Commander of British Troops Egypt: "Jumbo" Wilson. Though I had been told it was a volunteer-only mission, I was interviewed when I arrived by Hermione Ranfurly, who wrote *To War with Whittaker*, and Mark Chapman-Walker. They told me that whether volunteer or not, I would be detailed to go. I quietly abandoned all resistance and quickly joined Fitzroy's party.

I ended up being in Yugoslavia longer than any other comparable British officer, having spent three intensive years, half of them as a member of the military mission to Tito's headquarters, and half in the Embassy in Belgrade, and living with the peasants in their cottages in Bosnia, Dalmatia, Serbia and for a short time in Macedonia. I talked a reasonably fluent Serbo-Croat and had been nearer the grassroots than had most of my contemporaries.

In his advance on Russia, Hitler's armies cut through the Yugoslavs, and particularly the Croats, like a knife through butter. The Nazis moved south and the Yugoslav army crumpled. In no time the war was over for them, though perhaps the delay it caused in the attack on Russia was eventually of some real importance.

The King and government fled to London, and Hitler divided the country amongst his allies. Puppet governments were established in Serbia under the Chief of Staff, General Nedic, who became an eastern Marshal Petain, and in Croatia, where the Italians sponsored the appalling Ante Pavelic. Each had their equivalent of the Waffen SS, Nedic's under a man called Ljotic, while Pavelic's were the Ustachi, the Croatian SS. The latter, clad in black uniforms, threw themselves with hardly a pause into the welcome task of killing Serbs, communists, Jews, gypsies, and any other enemies they could identify. They were strong and venomous, and specialised in burning churches. Thousands of prisoners were taken and an extermination camp established at Jasenovac where scholars now estimate that at least 200,000 were murdered.

In Serbia there was, with defeat, a short pause, but in the summer of 1941 news began to seep through to British intelligence that there was fairly determined resistance. The rising seemed to have started in the first place as a peasants' revolt against the invader in the traditional Serbian style. The first news came by roundabout means to the Yugoslav government in London. It appeared that a group of officers, peasants and farmers had banded together and taken to the woods. Under a Yugoslav army staff officer, Colonel Draza Mihailovic, they collected and captured arms, and linked up with other resistance bands.

It was not long before there was contact with the communist party whose leader newly appointed by Moscow, Tito, called for a rising after the attack on Russia by the Germans. A proclamation was sent around the towns and villages of Serbia by the partisan committee in Belgrade, urging Serbs to revolt. Many, mainly peasants and intellectuals, answered the summons, and joined Tito in the Western Sumadija. Here were formed the first partisan Odreds, whose first commander was Koca Popovic, an intellectual who had risen to the rank of general in the Spanish Civil War. These Serbian Odreds provided the basis on which were formed the first partisan brigades. Round these brigades grew the whole Janl, of which the Serb brigades, two of which retained their purely Serbian identity, were always regarded as its finest troops.

The first group of royalists, officers, and their supporters took the traditional name, from resistance days, of Cetnici – Cetniks. When they announced their rising the communists and their supporters styled themselves partisans. At first there seems to have been little difference between them and co-operation began naturally. They came, however, from different origins, possibly the most likely to be mutually hostile. The Cetniks were mainly officers and Serbs, the richer peasants, and Serbian nationalists, hoping to restore Yugoslavia through and under the leadership of Serbia; the partisans were intellectuals, members of a party proscribed under the pre-war government, workers and poor peasants and their leaders intended to recruit into an army which would aim to help the Soviet Union in their war against Germany. The Cetniks were traditional, their discipline tended to be loose, and their hopes fired by Serb nationalism. For the partisans, military discipline was more unfamiliar and they made it considerably tougher to ensure that the peasants, upon whose support they depended, were not antagonised by theft, vandalism, or sexual laxity by their troops. To begin with there were agreements, and joint operations, but basic incompatibility of the two groups soon became painfully apparent. In British terms it was rather like expecting the Guards Club to co-operate with communist party headquarters.

Despite Mihailovic's reservations, the first, mainly joint, attacks were launched in the summer and autumn of 1941, and met with considerable success. The Germans were stung into fierce reprisals; Hitler, as an Austrian soldier, had the prejudices of his kind who historically had often been at the throats of the Serbs. Prisoners were taken by the Germans and hanged or shot in prosperous Serbian towns. These massacres appeared to achieve the desired result of convincing Mihailovic of the permanent damage likely to

left:
Members of the British military mission attached to the partisan army, Bill Deakin centre, J.H. right, Lola Ribar between, November 1943.

below:
Waiting for an aircraft to land and take off the delegation to Italy, Glamoc, November 1943.

be done to Serbia and its population by the continuance of massacres on such a scale. Mihailovic and his commanders decided that, as there seemed no prospect of allies coming in the near future to the rescue, it would be wiser to retire to the mountains and woods and suspend further attacks until the chances of rescue or help on a large scale seemed nearer at hand.

Conferences between Cetniks and partisans were held to deal with these problems, at Tito's insistence. Some measure of agreement was reached, but clashes occurred for which both sides were responsible. By the late autumn the Cetniks had decided on a quiescent policy. Tito, on the other hand, who had become more suspicious of his allies and of their aims, had decided that his best course was to step up the fight and seek more recruits in the poorer and more deprived parts of the country. He therefore moved into Bosnia and Montenegro, where the atrocities of killing and burning on the part of the Ustachi had antagonised the local population and particularly the tougher Serbs who live outside Serbia. They were looking eagerly for some resistance group to join and help them to seek revenge for the loss of their houses, friends, and often families. Tito's activity and readiness to fight attracted many recruits, while Mihailovic's inactivity caused at least a part of his adherents gradually to melt away and push off home. Some of the Cetniks joined the Germans and joined in the general attack. The balance between the two movements was in a short time beginning to change and the partisans were becoming stronger and more numerous, and perhaps more desperate, than were the Cetniks.

Until 1943 the British knew only of the Cetnik resistance through the Yugoslav government, which had promoted Mihailovic to General and made him Minister of War. First, however, Captain Hudson and later Colonel Bailey had quickly penetrated to Mihailovic's headquarters, had met Tito, and had reported on this rather confused situation. London was also aware that another resistance group was also in the field. Most of the information came from German sources: signals, operational reports, and even Ultra traffic. It was clear that some major operation was in preparation in Montenegro where it appeared that the Germans and their allies were grouping considerable forces to quickly snuff out the partisans.

With no outside support coming to the Serbian partisans from other parts of Yugoslavia, SOE accordingly decided to send a mission to Tito and the partisans. So, during April and May 1943 three missions were dispatched.

Captain Hunter went to Croatia, Major Jones went to Slovenia, and Major Bill Deakin went directly to Tito. Bill had been a history don at Oxford, and had helped Churchill write his history of Marlborough. Churchill had not, however, been directly concerned with Bill's SOE work with Tito. Only after Deakin had turned up in Cairo to report to SOE after a trip to Romania, did he meet the PM who was also in Cairo. This fact was particularly important to Bill, who was sensitive to allegations that he had somehow been sent to Yugoslavia as Winston's friend.

So it was that Deakin was parachuted close to Durmitor with one companion, Captain Campbell, and a wireless operator, the splendid and versatile Yorkshireman Walter Wroughton, knee-high to a grasshopper. The country was mountainous, rocky and inhospitable, and completely exposed to air and other attack. The partisans were surrounded by German troops, including a crack mountain division, as well as by Italian and Bulgarian troops, and a large contingent of Cetniks. In the fifth offensive in Montenegro, Campbell was killed, and Deakin was wounded by a bomb which also hit Tito, an experience which served to establish a permanent bond between them. The partisans' situation was desperate, with many important figures wounded or ill. After fierce fighting they eventually withdrew over the Neretva River towards Bosnia with Milovan Djilas gallantly heading the rearguard in hand to hand fighting. Slowly the partisans made their way towards the new headquarters at Jajce, a mainly Moslem and Serb town. Just as they arrived, Tito called a Congress of the Regional Central Committees of the communist party, which established a provisional national government, the National Liberation Front, and conferred the rank of Marshal on Tito.

Deakin sent reports on the fighting to British headquarters in Cairo. When Churchill received these reports, he decided to give further consideration to the whole question of the British relationship with the resistance, and arrangements were made for new missions under Brigadiers Maclean and Armstrong. Fitz had been in the Long Range Desert Group of the SAS under my Cambridge friend David Stirling. Now he was to be sent direct to Tito, while Armstrong would be sent to Mihailovic. Both missions were given clear instructions to examine and report on the activities of their respective resistance movements, and in the case of Armstrong, to give Mihailovic certain targets to attack in order to prove whether he was prepared to give up his present passive attitude and engage in greater activity against the enemy. Our brief, in Winston's inimitable style was short and clear: find out whether partisan or Chetnik was the best resistance group to support; find out Tito's agenda; endeavour to mediate between Tito and Mihailovic; gain Tito's support for the return of the King; supply resistance groups; co-ordinate resistance operations with our own in Italy; evacuate their wounded.

We were trained near Alexandria, with many other SOE men who would be dropped elsewhere. Parachute training consisted of jumping off fast-moving trucks in the desert. As a preparation it actually did no good at all. If one was not crippled in this process, one was fit to go on a jump with a parachute. I was additionally handicapped by being told that I was to jump with a heavy piece of equipment: a beacon to attract other planes, from which on pain of death I was not to be parted. After other necessary training I climbed into an RAF Halifax at Bizerta on 27th September 1943. We flew in two planes to Bosnia, our head filled with lurid stories about the fate of trainees before us, such as George Jellicoe, an old Cambridge friend, whose parachute had failed to open and who was dragged along behind the plane until he could be winched back inside. There was also a story of a group of Greeks who all jumped out in order, but without their parachutes, and of a Coldstream guardsman, who jumped at attention in the proper regimental way, studiously keeping his fingers along the strip on the side of his trousers, but whose chute did not open.

Fitzroy, and Vivian Street – a promising soldier who had been assigned by Winston as the mission's chief military adviser – went in the first plane with Colonel Peter Moore, a senior sapper. They at once found the dropping ground properly marked by the partisans, but we missed it. Our crew were Australians at the end of their tour, and were thoroughly cheesed off by constant flying to Poland and elsewhere. After several hours flying across Bosnia and Serbia, the pilot realised we had missed the target, decided we were over Bulgaria and ought therefore return to Tunis. We tried again the next night and dropped successfully. My vital beacon, assiduously protected, turned out to be quite useless as no aircraft ever carried the counterpart equipment.

It is exciting and a little daunting to drop into occupied country with no real idea of what it is like or what is happening or, indeed, what to expect, for no one that any of us knew had ever done it. I knew nothing of resistance fighting, other than what I had imagined back at the Foreign Office or been told in Bari, where I had gone on my return from South Africa. I had a plan that in the event of Britain being invaded, I would run off to the Welsh hills with a little gun and try to join some resistance to an invasion. As for jumping, we had done our training in Palestine, with blue skies and flat ground, quite unlike that of Serbia. Moreover, as Mike Parker said years later: "Henniker was the world's worst parachutist; he could never learn to turn in the wind," which I thought was quite unfair.

I suppose we imagined extraordinary hardship and danger, an immediate hail of fire, getting lost in unknown country with bullets whizzing around, meeting people with whom one could not possibly communicate and who might well be hostile. If these were our thoughts, reality was very different. We were at once found, there were several people who could speak German and a few words of English, the partisans were recognisable as soldiers in serviceable uniforms and in familiar units: men and women together, for there was absolute equality in the army. We were whisked away to a small cottage with a spotless bedroom, large bed and a comfortable duvet and were given good food. Our baggage was collected and put onto an ox cart. Next morning we set off for Jajce, where Tito had his headquarters. On the way we had one of those curiously intimate and personal encounters with the enemy, so frequent in this sort of warfare; a tiny Fieseler Storch came droning over. The pilot took a long look over the side and carefully having looked us up and down, threw a couple of grenades towards us and our baggage. He missed.

I had been told by Fitz that I was to be his number two and chief political adviser; I was in fact a sort of general bottle washer and foreign affairs adviser, and became the bread and honey gatherer. Fitz, like me, was an amateur, and was in need of someone who was militarily more impressive. Thus he picked Vivian Street, like me from the Rifle Brigade, to be his actual second-in-command. In Jajce, Fitzroy and Vivian Street, who had landed before us, had had their first talk with Tito and were busy reporting to Cairo and London

The first task given personally by Winston to our mission, was to discover which of the resistance movements was fighting and killing the most Germans. This was really the sole criterion on which the government, in the person of Churchill, would decide which group to back and, of course, we could only report about the partisans. We were deeply suspicious of most of the stories we had heard. At the first meeting, Tito gave a good and full account of the actions in which his troops had been engaged, but this obviously required direct observation by our mission as to how the partisans had been involved.

As for Tito himself, there were at the time, and perhaps have always been, many extraordinary stories, for he was always a very secretive figure. Some, including Evelyn Waugh, who was later a member of our mission, always insisted that he was a woman; others that he was of any possible and many impossible nationalities and backgrounds. Fitz's first impression of Tito, which we confirmed, was favourable. He was clear and decisive and, like few communist leaders, gave an impression of having an open mind and of being prepared to discuss any subject we cared to raise, with an appearance of spontaneity and frankness. He had a quick and clear mind and was able to talk to Fitzroy in Russian, or to me in German.

We had been told in the first place to seek to persuade Tito to co-operate and make common cause with Mihailovic. Tito said that when he had gone into the woods he had been prepared to agree to serve under Mihailovic, but this offer had been quickly rejected by the Cetniks. Since then relations were further soured by a lack of co-operation and of trust, or even of information, as well as of frankness and about what the partisans saw as untrustworthiness and betrayal by the Cetniks. For the present, Tito did not think that there was a basis or a readiness amongst his followers to agree to any formal or regular co-operation.

A connected concern was the assent of Tito to the return of the King to Yugoslavia. This was a particular concern of Churchill's, and was almost a quirk: Winston always liked Kings, however mouldy. Tito said that the return of the King could only be decided at the end of the war, and he was prepared to agree that it should then be put to the people. The King could come back now if he was prepared to come as an ordinary citizen or soldier, but not as King. We decided to drop the subject.

The main help we could offer the partisans was supply drops of ammunition and weapons. If there was a wind during a drop, the supplies could drift a long way. We were given gold coins to buy the necessary services, particularly pack horses, which we might need. Of much greater interest to the partisans was parachute silk, which replaced non-existent material for clothes. Small red parachutes brought our personal mail and any other excitement.

The main assistance the partisans could afford the allies was in distracting the Germans and Italians. The partisans managed to keep 20 German divisions occupied in Yugoslavia; such was the size of the country and the nature of the resistance. We were charged with co-ordinating partisan operations as far as we could with our own in Italy. Co-ordination, except in the case of large operations such as the destruction of a large bridge between Slovenia and Italy, in which Peter Moore played a leading part, was difficult because the essence of guerrilla operations is flexibility and speed, and the partisans were by definition spasmodic and opportunist. We agreed to do all we could but, with occasional important exceptions, it was difficult to achieve.

I tended to seek RAF help to attack small specific targets, such as a train in a station. The RAF would appear with one bomb strapped on to the plane, and they quickly learned and invariably managed to take the target out cleanly. On one occasion, prior to the liberation of Belgrade, I asked inadvertently for American support in Leskovac. The response from a friendly American General, Ira Eacker, was too large, less targeted, and resulted in a quite unnecessary overkill. I was expecting one plane; they sent over 20. They bombed Leskovac on market day. I had hoped that they had bombed the factories. In fact they bombed everything but the factories. It perhaps counts as my war crime.

The most important single function was perhaps the evacuation of partisan wounded to Egypt or to Italy. Mobility was the key to guerrilla warfare, and partisans could thus never carry a large, or indeed any, baggage train. In the nature of things many people were wounded and could only be moved in great discomfort in bullock carts, with an almost complete lack of medicine. Most operations, if necessary and if there was a doctor with us, as one New Zealander was, were done with a swig of slivovic. If captured by the Germans, the wounded were likely to be shot and the partisans did the same to the Germans unless they were important enough to be exchanged. British officers were strictly instructed not on any account to have anything to do with prisoners taken by the partisans nor to benefit from any intelligence they might bring, in case this might appear to condone this gruesome practice.

In fact the RAF did marvellous work in evacuating many hundreds of wounded and this gave a great boost to partisan morale. There was a Russian squadron of 12 Dakotas which operated under British command from Italy, and when they landed the Russians were apparently constantly afraid of betrayal and took off as fast as they could, while the British pilots operated in a calm, leisurely and quietly efficient way, waiting until they had packed in as many wounded as the plane could hold before taking off. The Russians, though they had normal Dakotas, seemed to regard them as a Soviet secret and would not allow the skilled British mechanics to help them with repairs if they damaged a plane on landing.

When I arrived as head of the partisan mission in Serbia, the partisans were desperately short of ammunition, having no more than 15 rounds per weapon, and many of those were defective. If only to raise morale when confronted with an enemy equipped with mortars and artillery, the partisans also needed some heavier weapons, as well as clothing: Uniforms gave them a higher standing in the eyes of the peasants and did something to offset the enemy propaganda that they were merely robber bands.

The months of May and June 1944 perhaps saw in Serbia the most remarkable change ever wrought by Anglo-American supply in the whole of Yugoslavia. It was a complete triumph for our system of air supply. The partisan organisation in Serbia was developed into a well-armed army of five small divisions with reserves of ammunition for all weapons. More than 10,000 men were armed, and sufficient heavy mortars were provided to give the partisans some answer to the heavier weapons used by the enemy.

Having completed our first contacts in Jajce the next task was to see as much of the fighting as we could. Fitzroy decided that he and I should go to the Dalmatian coast and islands to arrange for supplies to be brought in by sea, as the retreating Italians had left a gap on the coast. On our way down to the coast, we met Deakin returning in a farm cart from Split, where he had witnessed the handing over by the Italians of a very considerable accretion of arms to the partisans. Their acquisition alone transformed the ability of the partisans to wage war. In a crowded Split, with the Italians anxious to go, and the partisans anxious that they should go, Bill and Popovic took the Italian surrender.

Bill gave graphic accounts at the time and also in the *Embattled Mountain* and his later writings, of the operations in which he had been involved and of his relationships with the partisans and was naturally our main source of personal observation of the methods, personnel, and operations of the partisans, and of their breaking their way out of Montenegro to Bosnia. It had been a very difficult undertaking. It was the first time I had really spoken to Bill, and from that moment we became close and trusting friends. There was claimed to be a sort of jealousy between Bill and Fitz. They were both friends of mine, and always got on very well with each other, but the rumour was spread that Bill was not delighted that he had arrived first, had done all the work, and then Fitz received the credit. I actually think Bill's experience of and involvement in the fighting left him exhausted for the rest of the war.

Fitzroy and I moved on to the coast to Baskovoda. There we took part in the first liberation celebrations in Korcula. Over 50 years later I still have the hangover. We were taken from village to village, and in every village were offered a tot of the local brew to toast every good cause. We were very impressed at the first village by a guard of honour who was the very model of a proper partisan. He was a dramatic character with a thick, black moustache, riding a beautiful black horse, who drew a sword to salute us and shook our hands. We were even more impressed when a similar figure repeated the ceremony at the next village, though neither he nor the horse looked quite as mettlesome as those at the first village. It was a process that repeated itself at every village, but each time the man and horse that greeted us looked wearier and wearier. Then the truth dawned on us, through the haze of the local plum brandy: we were being welcomed to every village, without a flicker of recognition, by the same man who was galloping ahead of us. I wondered many times whether he had survived the war. He had. Forty years later, when I appeared on Fitz's *This is Your Life*, the horseman had been discovered, living in Dubrovnik: his name was Malina Ante.

On Korcula, Fitz and I also attempted to contact the Royal Navy, though without immediate results. When a German flying boat bombed the harbour, and the Germans began to return along the coast road of the Peljesac peninsula, we decided that, with telegrams arriving from the Commander-in-Chief and Churchill, it was time to return to Jajce and arrange for the dispatch of the first partisan mission to the allies.

Fitzroy was urgently needed at a conference to decide future policy with the resistance movements. It was also agreed that Tito should send a delegate to meet Churchill and the allies in Italy.

The first attempt to get them off Jajce was abortive. A Croat Heinkel flew over to the partisans with its crew from Banjaluka and landed at Livno where I had been left as head of our mission in Serbia. We informed Jajce, where Bill Deakin, after discussion with Tito, telegraphed to Italy that in view of the urgency of getting a mission to Italy and the difficulty Fitz and the RAF were having in landing an aircraft to pick them up, it might be worth considering the use of the Croat aircraft. This was agreed, and after some vicissitudes I got the aircraft to take off from Livno to the landing strip at Glanmoc, some 10 miles away.

The Yugoslav party, Deakin, and several British officers had come down from Jajce overnight and were at the landing strip. When the Croat aircraft arrived and was, with engines running, about to take off, Deakin and some others looked up, saw a small German aircraft fly over, and a bomb bouncing towards them. It did no harm to the first person out of the plane, Tony Hunter, but as it bounced on it blew up and killed Robin Wetherley and Donald Knight, an engineer. Deakin was so small that the blast went over his head and did him no harm and did the same to his wireless operator who was even smaller. The bomb also killed Lola Ribar and severely wounded the other partisan, Milojevic, a member of the mission. Ribar was the outstanding young communist of the coming generation, and a close confidante and friend of Tito. His death was probably the worst blow, for he was unique, on account of his age and intelligence, in the communist party, and the gap he left was never filled, to the future detriment of the development of Yugoslavia. Deakin and the rest, except for one of the Yugoslav mission, Miloje Milojevic, a heavily decorated solder, were untouched. The party withdrew, and some days later the rest of the mission were picked up by the RAF and Fitzroy landed safely in Italy.

It was subsequently suggested that the betrayal of the plane's movements to the Germans was the work of the plane's wireless operator, who was killed by the bomb after he had passed a message to the Croat and German headquarters at Banjaluka. This was, I believe, born out by the result of a committee of enquiry set up by the partisans to find the causes of the accident. This almost certain sacrifice of his own life would appear to reveal a fanaticism which was certainly not unknown amongst the Ustachi. For example, once, outside Kupres, I came upon the grisly sight of a whole company of Ustachi, who had blown themselves up with grenades to avoid capture.

It may seem peculiar nowadays to speculate that the partisans would have blamed the British for the disaster, since we were by far their most loyal and tolerant ally. A great many of them were always suspicious of us and, as now, ascribe all the ill-will towards the Serbs as being the result of some deep-laid plot between the Americans and ourselves to discredit them, but I really do not think that there was one jot of evidence which could have implicated the British in this disaster. Their concerns were pure melodrama as so much Ustachi thinking was. Stories were rife in Livno which was deeply anti-partisan. It was a Roman Catholic town where the Franciscan priesthood was active and hostile and where the women were deeply religious in a false, frightening way.

By this point I was sent as head of mission to the headquarters of the Dalmatian Corps at Livno. I had been warned by Fitzroy that if the decision was taken to transfer our aid from Mihailovic to the partisans I should take charge of a new mission and go either overland with the partisans to Serbia, or return to Italy to collect another mission and fly on to Serbia.

After some fighting along the Dalmatian coast behind the Dinaric Alps I received my orders to go to Tito's headquarters at Drvar, where he was soon afterwards attacked and very nearly captured in a cave by German paratroopers. Once there I was told that a decision had been taken by Churchill to cease aid to Mihailovic and to transfer it to Tito. Hitherto, Tito had not been sent any supplies in Serbia, which had been regarded as Mihailovic's preserve. I was to go with all speed and get him arms as quickly as possible to help the partisans get operations going in Serbia. At Bosanski Petrovac I spent some time with Randolph Churchill, the Prime Minister's son, who had arrived on 20th January 1944, specifically charged with handling propaganda.

I was fond of Randolph, though he was undisciplined. He looked after me when I had paratyphoid. He talked a lot about his father, and had been with him at the Tehran conference with Stalin. He made it clear that Winston regarded Yugoslavia as very significant, though he had a rather possessive opinion of Tito. Randolph was particularly nice on his own, but when someone else arrived he would show off. I had to keep my distance from Randolph after the war when he kept importuning me for information from Ernie Bevin's Private Office after I had become Ernie's Private Secretary.

We made an airfield in the snow in order to fly out to Bari, and then we danced on it. We were picked up by Squadron Leader John Selby, our RAF adviser, by Whitney Straight, the rich and well-known American who had volunteered for the RAF, and a New Zealand pilot. All went well, except that John Selby thought that in fairly deep snow we were not going to get off, and terrified us by yelling at the pilot.

On 15th April we returned. With me were two other missions under Majors Armstrong and Saunders, and an ISLD mission under Squadron Leader Syers. There was also Lieutenant Colonel Lynn (Slim) Farish, an American, there to represent the United States as they fancied a bit of secret war. Slim intended to return on foot to partisan HQ in Bosnia. He had originally joined the British army before the United States had entered the war, and was transferred to the British mission to join Fitzroy. Later he left me to report to President Roosevelt in Washington, and was later killed when his plane crashed on the way to Greece.

Slim and I were always apparently in complete agreement, but, before he left for Washington, he warned me that it was not popular with his supervisors for him always to tell the same story as me. I fully accepted this, and that American interests were often slightly different from ours. I was a little surprised after the war that his reports after he left me, seemed to indicate that there were serious differences between our interpretations of partisan/Cetnik relations. I never had any indication of this at the time, and we were close friends.

Slim and I were parachuted to Major Dugmore, a Rhodesian, who had had a hard time without supplies of any kind, under the snow all winter, in a strongly Cetnik area annexed in the war by the Bulgarians. Our drop was near Vranje in the Sar mountains, and Slim got slightly injured. Having never received any planes or supplies, Dugmore was determined that we should find him, so he put his fires on the very top of a mountain and we all had pretty nasty landings with our parachutes spread over many miles. Nevertheless, Dugmore was hugely relieved to see us.

Dugmore had with him Frank Thompson – brother of E.P. – a young and idealistic communist poet who had just come down from Oxford, where he had been expected to marry Iris Murdoch. I did not at the time know Frank was a communist; he was far less obtrusively so than people I had with me at times, and in fact seemed unusually objective. We were all genuinely operating a non-political directive. Frank Thompson was heading the only SOE mission to the Bulgarian partisans who looked a very unsavoury lot. Frank had had a horrible time and was exhausted. No one helped him from Cairo and he was discouraged. In the previous week he had lost his head of mission, Major Mostyn Davies, who had been killed in an ambush by Bulgarian troops. Frank had escaped only by running very fast. When I met up with him, he was so tired that one night when we had a move he fell asleep on the march and fell off a cliff into a river.

Frank had suddenly been saddled with the whole responsibility, and had to put up a constant fight to avoid being taken over by the Yugoslavs and to steer a middle course between this and being led off on a lunatic expedition with the Bulgars. There was still no clear policy. I met the Bulgars with him and formed the impression that I was glad they were not my prop and stay – compared to the Yugoslavs they had an unreal and slightly comic air of a brigand army, boastful, mercurial, temperamental and with an inexperienced yen to go it alone.

Shortly after I left, Frank decided to go into Bulgaria. There, on 31st May, he was captured and on 5th June, he was executed by the Bulgarians. The decision had been taken under martial law ostensibly by a local police captain, but in all probability with the sanction of someone much higher. He had made such an impression on the local people, that they erected a memorial to him in a village named in his memory: Thompsonovo.

In great contrast to Frank was Evelyn Waugh, who was dropped in with Randolph to Croatian headquarters. I did not like Waugh at all, and he was a disaster in the Yugoslav context. He was a little older, and very acerbic. In his *Sword of Honour* trilogy however, he captured, in a very real way, many of my experiences. The final novel, *Unconditional Surrender*, was in places almost directly autobiographical for us in Yugoslavia. Throughout his time there, Waugh kept in touch with his people back home. He was a well-read Roman Catholic, and a crashing snob. He professed to be interested in Yugoslavia, though he loathed the partisans because they were all anti-Catholic, communists and peasants. He was also interested in Fitzroy, as Fitzroy was in him. Waugh was, like Randolph, John Clark and Andrew

Maxwell, junior military attachés, and indeed all of us, useful to Fitzroy. We served as markers on the board, and it gave the mission prestige and a higher profile back home, and added to the impression that Fitzroy had a lot of people on his side. Waugh was not much practical use to Fitz, however, because he could not bring himself to talk to any of the partisans.

I returned to Serbia and the next few weeks were very active. Korca Popovic, commander of the partisan First Corps, joined us in southern Serbia, with a Russian mission. We very quickly brought in enough arms to equip five new partisan divisions, though not all were of high quality. We departed southwards to the Albanian border pursued and harried by Bulgarians, Germans, Albanians, and Serbian puppet troops. The Russian mission lost no chance of belittling the partisan effort and strength. From the start they were personally very friendly towards us, and expressed a strong desire to co-operate closely with us. As usual, however, having pumped us for all the information we had, they gave us very little in return, usually merely repeating somewhat inaccurate information we had already received directly from the partisans. I believe that this was largely due to the fact that they were given little information by their headquarters. For Russians, they indeed showed surprising confidence in us by asking us to pass messages for them in their own cypher when their wireless communications failed.

This was the only time in my service in Yugoslavia when the partisans quite shamelessly let us down. They panicked, ran away and left me with the pack ponies, women and children, whom I had to lead away and eventually shepherd back to the main force. The local partisans were equally undisciplined in a night march over the then Albanian border, when, with absolute silence an imperative, the children shouted and screamed a lot and brought down mortar fire on us all.

The departure of the British officers who had been working with Mihailovic until the new directive to help only the partisans, was very honourably arranged by Mihailovic, who could hardly have been criticised if he had refused to help them leave Yugoslavia. The transfer of our support to the partisans was a very difficult decision, which has been the subject of very harsh criticism, mainly from British and American sources, since the war. It has been condemned as a gratuitous folly to help a communist regime to achieve power against every British interest and as a disgraceful betrayal of our old friends and allies, the Serbs.

I object to the charges of dishonesty against Fitzroy, and even more to those against Bill Deakin. We all acted totally honestly to carry out the instructions we were given. The idea that we, the British, made Tito and glued him forever onto Yugoslavia's neck is exaggerated and overweening. Tito was active all over the country and the Cetniks were basically in Serbia. Tito never seemed to us at that time the perfect solution, but, rather, the best of a necessarily imperfect solution.

I have never had any difficulty in accepting that the decision, though perhaps unpalatable, was in fact the right, and, indeed, the only decision we could take. Mihailovic was trapped by his decision to suspend resistance, which allowed many of his troops to melt away and for the morale of those who remained to seep away. He himself seems to have been obsessed by fear of unnecessarily endangering Serbian lives, and could not stir himself out of inertia. I have always seen him as a wholly honourable man and soldier and have never thought he collaborated directly with the enemy. His chief mistake was, I believe, that he took direct responsibility and credit for the actions of unreliable, rather disreputable, and disloyal Cetnik commanders who openly consorted with the enemy and were even decorated by them.

It would have been worse, then and now, if Mihailovic had been successful, for he and his followers were all Serbian nationalists with little time or respect for other ethnic groups. When I was in Serbia I heard lots of reports from local Serbs of indiscipline, drunkenness, and licentious sexual demands, and even rape, by the Cetniks. I always scouted these, for the Serbs, like many other people, tend to tell one what they think one wants to know, and I was patently with the partisans, where sexes were more or less segregated and sexual intercourse firmly discouraged: the partisans could not afford to carry pregnant women or risk depletion of their army. But, as these reports have now been echoed by all we hear of the present Cetniks, I have, late in the day, come to believe that they were probably true.

Between our arrival in the autumn of 1943 and the decision being taken in the spring of 1944, some important facts changed, and it really was no longer in our power to decide on the outcome, or even to influence it. The assumption is always that we came into a situation existing on an even playing field. In fact, when we arrived, Tito was in the ascendant. The Italian collapse and the acquisition of large amounts of arms, however poor, by the partisans had greatly tilted the balance of strength in their favour.

They had fought the Germans steadily and attracted recruits where Mihailovic had decided after a blood-stained start, to lie lowish. By then, the rumours there had been about possible British landings in Dalmatia were known to be false and clearly we were not to be involved in the final act in Yugoslavia. I was with the Bulgarian army when it came into Yugoslavia with the Soviets at Nish. The Red Army was now closing in on Belgrade, and would be the major factor in the outcome. It seemed better and wholly in line with Winston's policy, however difficult it may in fact prove to be, to try and co-operate with them, than to fight a rearguard action which at that stage stood no chance of success and could greatly damage other interests of ours.

I think the bitterness of the attacks on British policy and suggestions of betrayal of Serbs and Cetniks were harmful. The historical revisionists of the Beloff, Amery, and Lees school have got wide support for their belief that we were politically motivated or misled to hoodwink Winston. While the injustice of some of the claims that those of us with the partisans were politically or otherwise biased were wholly unfair and do not much matter, they stoked the bitterness about betrayal which is always near the surface of Serbian minds. The Serbs moreover resented their failure to emerge with a better reputation and more gains from the war, and were, for that reason, though perhaps only to a small extent, contributory to recent violence.

I believed we exactly and conscientiously carried out to the best of our ability the tasks we were specifically set by Winston, and did not misinform him seriously, though perhaps occasionally being a bit too credulous of the partisan gloss on their actions. Though our relationship with the Russians once they came into the war involved notable disadvantages, Winston – on advice rather than his own inclination – took absolutely the only line we could follow in the circumstances in which we found ourselves, both over the war in general and over our involvement in Yugoslavia in particular. The military strongly advised him that the partisans were of more use to them, as our reports suggested. Nothing else was feasible and it is all very well for those who come *ex post facto* on the scene to believe that we were operating on a *tabula rasa*. Only the extreme and malevolent right-wing Serbs now believe we were wrong. There will always be people about, particularly in Serbia, who want to question the integrity of others. I personally have no doubts and no conscience whatever about what we did.

From the return of Koca Popovic's forces from the south, the war moved fast to its conclusion in Yugoslavia. The partisans were engaged in a rather half-hearted effort to help us to block the German withdrawal from Greece. Tito disappeared from Vis to visit Stalin and Marshal Tolbukhin arrived on the Romanian front. Churchill was furious: "Tito has levanted" he telegraphed, and he demanded that Tito had to be found. I leapt on a horse in the Redan in Serbia to go and find this levanting fellow. I knew exactly where he was: he was with the Russians at the Romanian frontier, where he made an arrangement with them about the capture of Belgrade, first by the partisans, followed by the Russians. I rode through the night and found Popovic and the others, but not Tito.

Tito's trip was presumably to report on his position, and to plan the details of the liberation of Belgrade by Soviet and partisan forces. I was always, even at the time, amazed that Winston seemed to think that after he had deigned to meet him, Tito should be his faithful supporter, even stooge. It seemed to me perfectly obvious that Tito saw himself as a free agent able to pursue his relations as he saw fit with the allies, and especially with the Russians – his original protectors. It also always seemed to me clear that he would do so, even if that was disappointing. Yet I was sent chasing round Serbia hunting for Tito to try to get him to come back to Vis, or to abandon his perfectly logical effort to negotiate the manner in which the Red Army would enter and operate in Yugoslavia. After all, Tito was never anything other than a dedicated communist.

Popovic was, to his chagrin, not allowed to take Belgrade and we were shunted back to Nis with the unpopular Bulgarians. Belgrade was taken quickly and the Soviet and partisan forces marched off toward Austria and Central Europe and the end of the war. The military mission worked hard at clearing up the unsatisfactory and eventually abortive and unsuccessful business of arranging the return and participation in government of the government-in-exile under Dr. Subasic. They were formally included in Tito's provisional government in powerless positions and were subsequently disqualified from the first elections. We busied ourselves with securing the appointment of three regents to see that the King's interests were considered at the end of the war. They did not, or were not allowed to, attempt to do anything on the King's behalf. It was hardly a triumphant end to years of hard and frustrating work.

SEVEN

Belgrade, 1945 and 1946

Before the military mission completed their task and left, I was recalled to the Foreign Office and, in spite of an almost tearful request for a change, was asked, and naturally accepted, a challenge to return. My mission was to make ready the Embassy in Belgrade for the first Ambassador, Sir Ralph Stevenson, then Ambassador to the exiled government in London. The Permanent Secretary, Sir Orme Sargent agreed that I should be given a platoon of Welsh guardsmen and a junior officer to tackle the task. We had to clear up the mess in the Embassy where the belongings of the British, who had had to leave when Belgrade was first attacked by Hitler, had been deposited, and which had been fought through and over.

VE night, 8th May 1945, was marked by a great party with the Americans at our Embassy. This was followed by a sort of drumhead court martial for our carousing soldiers who had been in fights with the Russians and had been involved in abstruse black market operations and the stealing of Embassy cars and supplies. Most of the Ambassador's silverware had disappeared; Toby Millbanke, an honorary attaché, at the Embassy who had been with us that night, had been hit on the head by the Russians, and died without ever being quite the same again. Two of the defence attachés had been, without our authority, flying out their girlfriends and then their girlfriends' relations. It was all the inevitable consequence of the Balkan life we were living: the type of war we had been fighting had corrupted our men.

I had been demobilised in early 1945, and on my twenty-ninth birthday, was immediately posted as Second Secretary to our Embassy in Belgrade; or, rather, to open the Embassy in Belgrade. Our relations with the Tito government, which was to last for 35 more years, rapidly deteriorated. Fitzroy was able to leave on a reasonable note as the liberation celebrations began to peter out, though he told me later how glad he was to leave when he did and not to have to share our frustrations. Discipline was pretty bad. For me, as the forerunner of the Embassy, there were many tasks. I spent much of my time with my Welsh guardsmen clearing the left-behind furniture, mending the heating system and the damage to the building, engaging staff, all of whom were ponderously vetted by OZNA, the secret police. and collecting food, such as sucking pigs, and other supplies from my peasant contacts. We also had to settle into the routine of life under communism, routinely hearing heavy breathing by the butler at the keyhole, noting the searching and removal of the contents of all the wastepaper baskets, telephones being bugged and every move outside the Embassy being carefully shadowed. I usually escaped by moving faster than my pursuers.

We had an excellent and reasonably well-informed staff. Bill Deakin returned, having been appointed First Secretary – my boss – prior to going home to redeem a pre-war promise to return to Wadham College, Oxford. Bill was the great strength of the Embassy. His knowledge of the odd factions of the Yugoslavs were of great value to Stevenson, when they impinged on the high politics centred around Trieste. Despite this, Bill was a bit suspect on the refinements of the internal scene: political oppositions and the like, which was the sphere of myself and Stephen Clissold. Bill had missed the more routine period after the fifth offensive, and did not speak the language well enough.

I felt a strong sense of the failure of any hopes we had had. We were told that the Big Three Conference at Yalta had agreed Western and Eastern spheres of influence, and that Yugoslavia was to be divided equally between the two. On the ground it looked nothing like that, and produced what appeared to be a concerted campaign of harassment against us. It was only too clear that Tito saw the Russians as his old friends and masters, and was dutifully fulfilling the commission he had been given and had so successfully performed in reforming the communist party and handing it back to their charge. I had hopes, not, I think, shared by Fitzroy, that Yugoslavia might be common ground on which we could at least collaborate with the Russians. After his time in Russia, Fitzroy was always deeply sceptical about productive co-operation with the Soviets.

Relations with the Yugoslavs went into a steep decline over Trieste, which had been established as a free territory administered by ourselves, the Americans in the north, and by Yugoslavia in the south. The Yugoslavs tried to steal as much as they could of the city, and our officers were obstructed, subjected to hostile propaganda, frustrated at every turn, and were even detained and prosecuted. When we complained to Tito, he was genuinely shocked, said it was all a mistake, and the particular incident stopped, only to be followed by another. It was clear that, in the Yugoslav communist party, there were Brownie points for bullying the British, and, though general directives were issued, even junior officers harassed us as much as they wished or thought wise.

Everywhere I went I found echoes, though less feverish and in a lower key, of the worst abuses I had first experienced in Germany before the war. Despite memories of individual outrages, there was never a feeling against Muslims comparable to that against Jews in Hungary and Poland. "Spontaneous" demonstrations against ourselves and the Americans were frequent, followed by a steady round of war crimes trials. As one of the only moderately fluent speakers of Serbo-Croat, my job was to attend these routine trials and to witness what amounted to a deliberate attempt to humiliate and destroy the small middle class. The often trivial charges, and the hectoring of the judges, were sickening. The charges were usually associated with collaboration, be it treason, espionage, or material or moral assistance to the enemy. Information was also requested against those who had any connection with the concentration camp at Bubanj, where the Germans were alleged to have murdered some 12,000 Serbs. In both Nis and Leskovac, the partisans did not appear, on the surface, to take too harsh a line.

In Nis there were stated to have been around 1,000 arrests in the first 10 days, but there were no reports of many being shot, and the town was always regarded by the partisans as being one of the most strongly collaborationist in Serbia. Doubtless there were many cases of wrongful arrest, drunk as the partisans were with success, and with their first taste of power. Moreover, in Serbia, there had not as elsewhere been free territory which included towns on which the partisans could cut their administrative teeth. On the contrary, the whole area was liberated suddenly, and the totally inexperienced partisans were left to cope with the situation. That they made any show at all was to their credit.

I have no great opinion of the Serbs, except for some as individuals. Serbs were the least reliable troops I ever fought alongside. With the army, they became top dogs at the end of the First World War and did little to deserve it; but they have assumed it to be their automatic right and have fought their way back to reassert it. They share with the other Turkish ex-colonies, as I experienced in the Arab world as Ambassador to Amman, an obsession with weapons, and with using them irresponsibly. They are hopelessly bad with them, inaccurate, and determined that they need no guidance.

When I got to Serbia the Cetniks had been hanging about for a few years dressed in fanciful military gear. Inactivity and guilt made them boastful, unreliable, and, as they usually tend to be quarrelsome, undisciplined, oppressive, and licentious. They have a charm for which many British seem to fall, just as they do with Arabs. The many fearsome and picturesque qualities appealed to romantic writers from Rebecca West to the intrepid nineteenth century (often female) travellers.

The extreme nationalism of the Serb is certainly primitive, which is why I found it easy to accept our decision to back Tito over Mihailovic, as the underdog, whose personal courage I never doubted. Again, the British have found Mihailovic attractive, and have subsequently, in an attempt to re-write history, encouraged the Serbs to feel that they were unfairly treated; a situation they now feel justified in attempting to remedy. The small differences between Serbian and Croatian dialects (they would call them languages) have been an important component, perhaps the main rallying cry, in such insensate nationalism. I have in retirement gone to Croatia, and found that my attempts to speak the language, though I tried to modify it to sound more like what I thought was the Croatian idiom and accent rather than the Serbian, made the Croats who heard me cool and suspicious, as if I sounded Serbian and was therefore biased towards Serbia.

I think we have sadly overestimated, from memories of the First World War, the reliability of the Serbs and their attachment to us (in which I was originally inclined to believe) on the lines of "gallant little Serbia". I doubt if that was wise, or a valid basis for our relationship with them. Brigadier Bailey, who was the senior officer with the Cetniks, said that the Cetniks did not do much good in the war because it was not the sort of war they most enjoyed or were traditionally used to conduct against the Turks. The Turks had always been accustomed to leave them a certain freedom if they did not interfere with their military communications.

For their part the Serbs kept up a tradition of resistance rather akin to a field sport with close and open seasons. One Serb told me the pattern. In the spring when the leaf came on the trees, they left the towns and villages for the woods which provided cover; they dressed in glamorous clothes, rifles, bandoliers, Komitadji caps, beards, knives, and such like, and would go and shoot the Turks when they came out of the pubs. Then the Cetnik would have themselves either drawn or photographed preferably standing over a fallen enemy with a gun or a knife poised for the *coup de grace*, and send the cards to their girlfriends. Other souvenirs, such as heads, they posted to the Sultan. In the winter as the days drew in, they took off their smart country clothes and went back into the pubs and drank with the Turks, until the spring came again. It was all a game, played all year round.

There are other pretty indelible traits in the Serb which were even more exaggerated in Montenegro: a sort of morbid preoccupation with appearances of honour, pride, retribution for weakness, supposed treachery, or fear, and no mercy or compassion for those held not to have come up to scratch. I remember in Montenegro going to a house where two sons had been executed for working with the enemy. It was like a Roman play, or a Corneille version of Roman virtue: the mother expressed warm approval of their fate. I always felt that this might be mainly show, but it does represent a characteristic which is, or was, fashionable and which they like to pretend to live up to as proper Serbs. Even to discuss redemption would have appeared unacceptably weak.

The Embassy sent me down for a longish period to Skopje to open the Consulate and act as Vice-Consul. While I was there I was quite often involved with Greece and Bulgaria, over which the first really serious disagreements with the Russians had begun to appear. I already knew some of the Macedonian government, and found them easier and more efficient to deal with than officialdom in Belgrade. I could never, however, go out in my Jeep without finding tyres deflated by a plentiful supply of three-pronged nails. The Macedonians too were disappointed not to have been better rewarded for their earlier assistance.

Another task for which I was useful was to keep abreast of how far the country was at peace, and of what appeared to be happening to the regime's opponents. Because I knew where I was going, I could get away before the secret police were wise to my intentions. I could thus outdistance them, and get to my destination and hear the news before, panting, they caught up.

Peter Carey, who later became a very senior civil servant, and who was always quick, well informed and steadily a great support, came to us in 1945 as an emergency Information Officer. I drove him round the country in a truck. The main object of our tour was to try to find out whether dissident Roman Catholics – the Krizari – existed, and where the Cetniks and Mihailovic might be found. We had heard much of these resistance movements in Belgrade, but we were in the main deeply suspicious of these stories. The Krizari sounded the most likely, and their religious provenance made them seem plausible. We went from Kosovo, to Mostar and the Sanjak of Novi Pazar and on through Bosnia to the Slovenian border looking for rumoured insurrections. It was an extraordinary journey, which I much enjoyed, as I went unimpeded to see people with whom I had stayed, and who then talked freely. Nearly everyone had heard of the Krizari, but by the time we reached the Austrian frontier they were still said to be in the next valley. It went on like that until the valleys disappeared over the frontier. In the end we decided that the only rather flimsy evidence seemed to show that there were probably a few bands in the Neretva area, but not much else.

We had heard that Mihailovic was in pretty impenetrable places. I started in Montenegro, went briefly to Novi Pazar out of historical curiosity and to see how things were in a place I did not know. Then, north to Hercegovina, Bosnia and Croatia and back to Belgrade. We were chiefly interested in Bosnia, but the excuse for my trip was calling in on the new governments and local authorities. Forgetful of the niceties of diplomatic manners, I met leaders of the opposition on dark streets or bridges, or more stealthily in their houses. Important contacts included the leader of the Serbian left-wing agrarians, Dragoljub Jovanovic, and members of the returned government-in-exile. All seemed strangely insular, confident of the strength and the eventual pressures of their local following in Yugoslavia to get them back into government, but unwilling to offend the communists by encouraging their allies, and feeling that the communists would have eventually to turn to them for help. Well before that day, most of them were totally neutralised, isolated, or actually behind bars.

Just after Christmas I set off on another freezing Jeep journey to my old stamping grounds to introduce Dugald Stewart, my successor, to my old contacts. We also did a run-around of Hercegovina and Dalmatia. The closing discussions in the military mission had been about a proper role for the King's Prime Minister, Subasic, and seeing the Regents in place at least, to provide formal assurance that we had done what little we could to promote the King's interests.

Looking back, I think that this was a time when it was essential for the new regime to make some attempt at healing and reconciliation if Tito's government were in the end to bring more peace to the country, rather than a semblance of order and calm which broke as soon as the pilot fell overboard. In the euphoria after victory, Tito would certainly have handsomely won a fair election, and it was not beyond imagination that some effort at reconciliation could have been successfully made.

I was surprised to find the partisans always so friendly and open towards us about how they saw the world. When we went to their headquarters the atmosphere of informality was extremely strange for a communist headquarters, much of it was very much like a British headquarters. There were comments and a good deal of chat even from the secretaries. The secretary at that time was Olga Nichic the daughter of the last Royal Yugoslav Minister of Foreign Affairs, who had been to Britain as a debutante. When I spoke to her she immediately asked me if I know the Monkey Club, a place where lone girls doing the Season in London stayed. Here was a remarkable sign that the atmosphere inside the headquarters was as it might be in one of our better units, and it gave me confidence that most of what went on behind the scenes amongst the partisans was not so deeply secret that we might not have heard about it.

Towards the end in Serbia, I was with Tempo, Tito's effective viceroy in the south and the outlying parts of Macedonia, when Radoslav Djuric, the leader of the south Serbian Cetniks, came over to the partisans. His troops mostly joined the partisans and were accepted. Tempo was out of contact with Tito and was seriously puzzled about what to do with Duric. He seemed to feel that he was under some sort of obligation and that even his honour was involved in Djuric being and being seen to be properly punished – even executed – for his activities in the war. Every night I sat on his bed and urged that the partisans would get far more credit from the world outside if they pardoned him and allowed him back to work his passage. Though always friendly, he refused to discuss the matter with me, presumably seeing it as unwanted interference. In the end, however, though Tempo never officially told me of his decision, Djuric was pardoned and became Chief of Staff. It made me happy that I had at least been able to save one important life.

In the spring of 1946 I left for London. By then the shoddiness of communist rule, of plodding and inefficient bureaucracy, petty corruption, increasing unfriendliness, and the absence of any appearance of warmth generated by our presence and help in the war, had brought me close to exhaustion and dark disillusion. I felt then, and for several years afterwards, almost totally exhausted and drained by the experience. For more than three intensive years there had been no let-up. From the end of the war we passed straight, without any break, into the Cold War of hostile Soviet propaganda, provocation, spying, and almost unbearable jargon: a world that was totally alien and the opposite of that which we had hoped to see. There was not a moment when we had a sense of victory, or even of success; merely the disappointment of hopes.

From the partisans, despite the formal award of decorations, there was little semblance of friendship or gratitude for our work. The issue of ethnic hatred was dodged, mainly due to the overwhelming sense of relief that the war was over. In this the country was pretty united, and no one wanted to jeopardise that unity by raising more problems. Almost immediately, many people in Britain, including Winston, were induced to feel that our policy had been wrong and was really better put in a back drawer. This attitude was responsible for our losing and failing to revive any real interest in that part of the world, apart from the occasional high-level exchange visits, between Tito and royals or ministers, until it was too late.

As a final disappointment, I found out, when I got back to London in 1945, bursting with news about the new country and the failings and more hopeful prospects of its regime, that my enthusiasm was not shared. Owing to trouble over Trieste, the Foreign Office were at last fed up with Tito's behaviour, and most of the interest in the new Yugoslavia had evaporated. I called on the Acting Head of the Southern department, Jock Colville, an old, old, friend of mine, as well as a relation, who had been Winston's Private Secretary during the war. He had kept me sitting in his office for half an hour, while he was writing what seemed to be a long memorandum. He then looked up briefly to say: "Pity we didn't back Mihailovic, wasn't it John".

EIGHT

Ernie, 1946 to 1948

As soon as Ralph Stevenson had climbed out of his plane to take over in Belgrade, I climbed in and flew back to London. My task in Belgrade had been formally completed. The war may have been over, but I remained deeply depressed at the lack of Foreign Office interest in Yugoslavia and in its apparent boredom with the success of our mission. I knew a great deal about Yugoslavia at that time and no one ever asked me for any views I might be able to express either then or later. Any chance I might have had of influencing what happened in the future, passed unnoticed. I had been offered, before I left Belgrade, the same sort of job that had been given to Fitzroy's staff; mainly to follow the remnants of fighting in Yugoslavia, and the various and varied numbers of Yugoslav refugees retiring northwards towards Germany, to help our forces sort them out and allocate them to the right sort of transit camps for appropriate repatriation. I felt, having lived through so many Yugoslav trials of their so called war criminals, mostly harmless men who had collaborated in order to save their families from persecution, I did not want to carry any part of this unpleasant business into a new life. I also felt very honoured and flattered to have been offered a job in Ernie Bevin's Private Office, which was to be my first real introduction to the workings of the Foreign Service.

It proved at first, difficult technically to arrange my posting in the Private Office, where life was very busy. When I eventually arrived, I felt very much at a loss, because I had never had anything to do with policy-making in the Foreign Office, experience which one ought really to have before taking up such a position so close to the Secretary of State, where obviously my advice would have been more useful if I had known the people he was dealing with. I was thrilled with the appointment, but felt uncertain about what contribution, if any, I could make. I regarded my appointment as reward for a war that was thought by the Foreign Office to have gone quite well. I had been badly wounded, and survived a hard time in Yugoslavia.

The Private Office was very agreeable, composed of old associates of Eden's with Bob Dixon in the lead, an appointment of genius because he and Bevin had a common Bristol background and Bob soon acquired Ernie's complete confidence. There was also Moly Sargent as Permanent Under-Secretary, Nicholas Lawford, my predecessor, and Nicko Henderson. I would be the Foreign Secretary's Second Private Secretary. The first; Dixon, wrote his speeches, and had the main contact with him. I was to be a sort of extra backup, a dogsbody keeping the arrangements straight, liaising with the Palace, and so on; improving the channels of communication between Ernie and the outside world. I felt at first like a fish out of water. I had come from a different world from the rest of them.

I was a rotten Private Secretary, but Ernie was always kind and tolerant. My colleagues were, from the outset, aware of my lack of experience and thought of getting rid of me after a bit; I do not quite know why, but I think they thought I was not quite settled, and some of the other members of staff were vaguely in love with my future wife Osla. I think Ernie had a sort of built-in view about me that I was from the aristocracy and was therefore likely to be a treacherous figure or one who inevitably would not understand the Labour party and its aims, from within his Private Office. I think it changed after I told him that Randolph Churchill had phoned me up in the middle of the night to find out what Ernie was thinking. I said, "If I did know, the last person in the world I would tell would be you, Randolph".

Ernie decided to keep me, but I did not become a great success. I tended to get my papers muddled, and I used to send him off to meetings that never took place. One day he came back from the Cabinet Office saying, "I went to Great George Street, but there was no one else there". I had got the wrong day. "Doesn't matter; wouldn't have been much fun anyway," he said. I wrote to my fiancée, Osla Benning, in August 1948, two years after my appointment: "I think I'm beginning faintly to understand what my job is all about at last, and I now occasionally have one or two thoughts, which, if not original, are at least my own after long and painful cogitation".

Ernie was a very good chooser of people who would work well with him. Oliver Franks, was the man that I admired most next to Ernest Bevin as the best public servant I have ever met. There were also many trades union leaders like Arthur Deakin and Sam Watson. Foreign diplomats: Massigli the French Ambassador, Lew Douglas the American Ambassador and Amr Pasha the Egyptian Ambassador were also close to Ernie.

Ernie's friends were often from different backgrounds, but they seemed always to work harmoniously together.

I always felt it was a bit of a cheek for me to speak to Ernie about politics, but he used sometimes to confide in me. It was a curious trait because he did not need to. Ernie's authority over foreign policy was I think absolute. Half the Cabinet were known to be his friends, and he had a very powerful position *vis à vis* the Prime Minister Clement Attlee. One morning, for instance, Ernie wrote a longish minute to Clem regarding our independent nuclear capability. He sent it off via an official messenger to Number Ten. It came back half an hour later. At the bottom, Clem had written: "I agree. Will support you in the House. C. R. A." This backing was all Ernie needed and he totally relied on it.

Ernie had a clear foreign policy: keep in with the Americans at all costs; keep in with everybody else; watch the Russians. Ernie's background was perfect for the Foreign Office, far more so than a Tory would have been at that time, because although anti-communist he could not be labelled as anti-Russian. He had been pro-communism during the revolution. He also knew communists very well, having had them at his elbow throughout his life. Winston, for one, always wanted to take Ernie with him when he saw Stalin, in the hope that he could be won round to being a friend of ours.

An area of deep trouble was Palestine, which kept rearing up and hitting us on the head. Ernie was thought to be pro-Arab, but I am not at all sure that he was: he in fact had every sympathy with the Jews. In a country which one half owned and the other half thought they ought to own, we had to keep the two races as far as we could operating on an equal playing field, where there was a lot of outside pressure, particularly from America, in favour of Israel. There was a tremendous row over the Exodus which was a ship full of refugees returning to the promised land with Ernie trying to be fair to both sides by restricting the number of Jews and Arabs allowed into Palestine. His only purpose was to try to be fair, as we, the British, had

Private Secretary to Secretary of State, Ernest Bevin, 1946.

undertaken to be under the mandate. Perhaps personally he had a very mild scent of the working man's anti-Semitism, but nothing remotely serious. He was determined to treat the Jews and Arabs exactly the same, but found this very hard in a deeply emotional atmosphere. For his trouble he was booed throughout America, which he visited for a meeting of the UN.

Ernie was more than anything else a problem-solver. On one occasion we had to send troops either through the Suez Canal, or round the Cape of Good Hope. Each choice presented problems. Ernie thought about it, and had an imaginative idea, which many thought impracticable, but of which I was strongly in favour. He thought we would avoid difficulties if we had a station in East Africa, and put troops there. We could then cut a road through the middle of Africa, and send the troops and communications in that way. An idea of genius, which the General Staff dismissed, quite typically, as a nincompoop notion which was only to be expected from a politician.

Ernie had great humanity, and could always feel empathy with those with whom we were dealing. He usually understood perfectly how foreigners would react to some action of ours. I remember driving back with him from the signing of the Dunkirk Treaty, on 4th March 1947. The Treaty was ostensibly directed at future German aggression, and marked an evolution in the development of Western co-operation, which was carried on through to the Marshall Plan and the Brussels Pact. Ernie suddenly said to me, "Henniker, I'm very glad we've done that; it puts France back at the high table; she'll be happier and easier to deal with". The Treaty was a success for Ernie as the French were being difficult all the time: I never imagined he was so sensitive to their worries about inferiority, or was likely to be other than irritated with them, as most of us were. Bidault, the Foreign Minister, was playing the *prima donna* as usual. The episode had the requisite farcical interlude, as I wrote from Berlin on 5th March 1947: "When we got to Calais, the cars to Dunkirk were already disastrously arranged and Dunbar, our Chef de Protocol, got lost with the Treaty, and the Secretary of State sat and fumed for half an hour with M. Bidault and no Treaty to sign". Dunbar, a First World War veteran had wandered off to have a look at an old battlefield.

With Europe, Ernie had some trouble. He got on well with Jean Monet, but was very offended when the French launched the Coal and Steel Pool without first consulting him in advance. Apart from the personal slight,

Ernie's entire career had been concerned with coal and steel production. He was prejudiced against the European ideal for a while thereafter. Our delayed involvement proved to be a very damaging stumble, and there were to be a great many more along the way.

Ernie's close friendships helped us enormously, and did much to bring about some remarkable things such as the Marshall Plan and the first outline of NATO. Ernie in fact came up with the idea for NATO. He never liked dealing with countries individually; he liked dealing with them in great swathes, where one could get them all in a room together. He was a geopolitical strategist by instinct rather than perhaps by intellect. The original Marshall Aid project did not seem very likely at the time. From modest beginnings intended to save Turkey, it came to cover all of Western Europe. Ernie had been warned in advance by the Americans that Marshall Aid was coming, and so had everything prepared when it did arrive. We hit the ground running and certainly ahead of the others. Ernie was also the motivating force behind the Berlin airlift, though the Americans took most of the responsibility, and the credit.

It was around this time that I began to realise something of my own interest and involvement in the wider political scene. I wrote to Os from Moscow in April 1947: "I like the way you assume that I'm desperately keen to go into politics. It's not really true, you know. It's only an idea I occasionally toy with to give me a feeling of independence when I'm thoroughly got down by the conferences of the Foreign Office." We had travelled to Moscow by train; Ernie could not fly for reasons of health. With our NKVD observers we went through Poland, and Ernie was absolutely horrified when he saw Warsaw.

Conferences were long and boring, but there could be compensations: "Sometimes, one does something quite amusing. We had a party in a Russian night-club the other night with the Austrian Foreign Minister, his party, two Austrian women and an extraordinarily tough French lady George Jellicoe picked up. She finished off the evening by making a pass at all of us in turn but she found no takers – not even George."

The Moscow conference in 1947 was deeply tedious and I wrote again to Os, "The conference drags on its languid length. No one has the foggiest idea when it will end, and everyone is beginning to hope it won't go on much longer." We were there to settle the peace with the Eastern Bloc. We did not get very far. It was a long affair, everyone was bored stiff, and the Russians were very difficult to deal with, particularly Molotov. Ernie thought Molotov was a dolt, and a bureaucrat of a particularly nasty order. As usual, the Foreign Secretary was frequently ill with colds of various kinds, and, exhausted, would appear to fall asleep during discussions. Then suddenly Molotov would make an absolutely unpardonable statement and Ernie would wake up and shoot the Russian down in flames despite not speaking Russian.

We were just waiting for one side to break. We visited the Kremlin: I suppose it was interesting, in a way, but we did not see much – the outside of churches, the state rooms, and two museums and most of us were pretty bored at the end. The state rooms are really horrors crammed with the worst type of Victorian bric-a-brac. Everything was unpleasant and faintly ominous. In a passageway one would hear a rustling and the sound of wind, and then the Russian delegation would sweep past very quickly, all wearing gym-shoes. I never knew why. Perhaps Stalin hated the sound of footsteps.

"Russians are so vague, and nothing works and generally I'm getting a bit fed up. I do so wish I didn't have to do these hateful and unsettling trips. One never can plan ahead, or work out what one wants to do ... I find that Conferences are the most wonderful things for making one either loath or love people. I have, I'm afraid, developed the deepest possible loathing for Alison David ... people like George Jellicoe and Laurie Humphrey [a Private Secretary to Attlee] are on the other hand a great stand-by. Either you live the diplomatic life *par excellence*, or you do nothing. Neither is quite my cup of tea."

Life got no better when I returned to the Foreign Office in July 1946: "Returning to this ghastly morgue brought back some of my worst doubts". In the morgue, Ernie worked very well and constructively with Bill Denning on the Far East, Harold Beeley on the Middle East, with Gladwyn Jebb, with Hall-Patch on European economics and, I think, also in this field, with Roger Makins who I always thought, as an intellectual, rather undervalued Ernie and never really understood his very special qualities of human understanding. They were people who could talk easily with him and from whom he got stimulation, while he brought out their best qualities. Bob Dixon had served as Ernie's Principal Private Secretary and had been marvellously successful. I wrote from Moscow in April 1947: "his successor will be Frank Roberts, who's Minister here, and is a ball of fire, very small and very good at everything, including games, and has a Syrian wife".

Outside the Foreign Office, Ernie was at ease with Herbert Gee, of the Ministry of Labour, and with Norman Brook, the Cabinet Secretary, and with Brian Robertson, over Germany. Brian had been Commander-in-Chief in Germany, and came with us to Moscow. He had considerable influence on Ernie, particularly considering that he was a soldier. They all worked well with and for him. No one, however, ever exerted undue influence over him. Under all circumstances Ernie was his own man, seeking to get knowledge and experience from the people he consulted but never necessarily to adopt their ideas.

With foreign statesmen I think his most remarkable friendship was with Dean Acheson. They somehow got on very well indeed and nothing could have been more different than their backgrounds; Acheson was an English gentleman transliterated to Connecticut. Ernie could not stand Acheson's dogmatic successor, John Foster Dulles, but then nor could anybody else. Ernie's liking for Schuman in France was also a considerable advantage but broke down, really, on what he regarded as the duplicity of Schuman in launching his plan about the Coal and Steel Pool without first informing him.

In the Private Office Bob Dixon and Nicko Henderson both were on his wavelength, and Nico, in particular was, at that time, in the Labour party and was rather a confidant of Ernie's. He has written a very good account of Ernie and the workings of the Private Office in *The Private Office Revisited*. Bob, who was a brilliant choice for his post, got on well with Ernie, not least because they were both from Bristol, where Ernie had actually delivered laundry to the Dixon household as a small boy. Pat Kinna was very close as Ernie's Political Secretary. Pat had been in the RAF, and was also an excellent shorthand typist, and was perhaps the only person in the world to have taken dictation from Churchill and Roosevelt while they sat in the nude in the bathroom of the British Embassy in Washington. Hector McNeil was a great friend who Ernie was guiding up through the Foreign Office, he was Ernie's ministerial number three at first and then became Minister of State until 1950. They were very close but he let Ernie down. Hector was not corruptible but he was open to influence. He had the great handicap of having Guy Burgess in his office, working with Fred Warner. Burgess appealed to Labour politicians who came to London with little idea of smart and decadent society. They were made to feel enormously in the know by chatting with Burgess, and he thus had easy access to the untutored Labour ministers. A lot of his gossip was bollocks, but some of it was true. Someone said at the time, that as soon as Burgess was told anything, "You'll hear that hoarse voice gassing away and it'll be round the Reform Club and round London in five minutes".

Burgess was a great nuisance in London and we were always trying to get him out, so we sent him to Washington and he became a worse nuisance there and they tried to get rid of him. He was always drunk and being stopped for speeding. He became an absolute pest, and was about to be removed when he heard from Kim Philby that his close friend Donald Maclean was under close surveillance, and thought to be a source of leaks of classified information to the Russians. He therefore left Washington the night before Maclean was to be interviewed officially, before being arrested. They vanished together from London in May 1951.

Ernie was a model of loyalty to Clement Attlee when Clem was Prime Minister, and sometimes had to be, in order to scotch intrigues from some of his more prominent colleagues. George VI had, after all, intervened to persuade Attlee to appoint Ernie as Foreign Secretary rather than Hugh Dalton. This was, I think, partly due to Louis Greig, who was a mutual friend of Ernie's and the King, and kept Ernie in touch with the Court. Ernie always firmly stood by Attlee who, I thought, was rather remarkable. I also thought it remarkable that Ernie's loyalty transcended the terrible private rivalry between Mrs. Attlee and Mrs. Bevin.

Ernie could attract strange bedfellows. Lady Cunard, a frightfully silly American socialite, and Lady Duff Cooper, and the Duke and Duchess of Bedford, had an idea that Ernie might be made the head of a salon, which would pick members of the government. It was a conceit from another century, the idea that they had political as well as social power, though it had occurred quite recently, in the relationship between Lady Londonderry and Ramsay MacDonald. As Ernie's Private Secretary it was hoped I would be the link. I thought it a totally potty idea from which I recoiled in horror. Even if they could get somewhere with Eden, they never would with Ernie. Perhaps they were misled by Ernie flirting with Diana Cooper, and his habit of pinching ladies' bottoms. Diana did throw parties for him at the Embassy in Paris, but nothing more ever took place. "This High Tory society was actually a world of make believe," I wrote to Os in August 1946.

"What a ghastly world people like Lady Cunard live in, trying all the time to pretend that they have the government in their pockets, and living way back, perhaps in Edwardian days, their only flutter in recent years having been *l'affair Simpson*, about which they talked a good bit. I see how the communists have a sort of vague case."

Ernie was at the centre of the government, and had his relationship with Clem not worked, the Ministry would have fallen apart. Ernie had common sense; one night when he was working in the office and I was the only Private Secretary on duty, Cripps and Dalton wanted to see him. They walked in looking terribly self-important. I went in after they had left. "I expect you would like to know, Henniker, what they were up to." I said, "I wasn't thinking of that Secretary of State". "Well," he said, "this is what they wanted. They wanted to push me up there. Torpedo Attlee. Make me Prime Minister. I'm having nothing to do with it. Nothing to do with it at all. They'll put me up there and do the same with me."

Ernie came to trust the Foreign Office; whether he came to love it is another matter. He felt at ease there; helped by those he liked, like Bill Denning, whom I had known in the Far Eastern department. Ernie quite liked Frank Roberts, who replaced Bob Dixon when Bob went to Czechoslovakia. Bob had done all the groundwork, made Ernie understand the Foreign Office; a remarkable feat, and accommodated the Foreign Office to Ernie's requirements. Frank was not a great Private Secretary: he tried to run Ernie as one of his subordinates who had to be told what to do. Ernie did not like to be told what to do. Every morning Frank would bring a list of things to do that day. Ernie would simply refuse to do them; Frank would badger him, so Ernie got rid of Frank, and sent him off to New Delhi in 1949. Nehru had said he had been left out by the Commonwealth Relations Office, and did not know what was happening in foreign affairs, and wanted to know about problems concerning India. Ernie placated him by offering his highly able Private Secretary as Deputy High Commissioner, to keep him in the picture. This both got rid of Frank, and kept Nehru on side.

Ernie always referred to his predecessor as "Poor Anthony". I think he was quite fond of Eden, but did not take him terribly seriously. I asked him once what he thought of a speech of Poor Anthony's. "Same old balls, clitch after clitch after clitch," he said, as he did often. Ernie thought Eden rather immovable; a correctly stiff-upper lipped Englishman forever resisting

Johnny Foreigner. Ernie thought there were rather too many of those in the Foreign Office, and did not think such people knew what they were talking about. I did not think they did, either.

My admiration of Ernest Bevin has never known any bounds. There was never a hint of dissemblance about him; he was a very open man. I have always admired him quite easily more than anyone else I have ever worked with. I genuinely believe that not only was he a man of splendid resolution, wisdom and common sense, but he was also in many ways something like a genius. I was always aware when working with him of what a privilege it was. With Pat Kinna I was often an observer to the most exciting events. Almost every day I found myself amazed at how versatile Ernie was. He was full of the most extraordinary and abstruse information. "Secretary of State, where did you get that information?" "Learnt it, my boy, in the 'edgerows of experience". And his experience was vast, particularly of all kinds and conditions of people. Somehow, in the most solemn discussion about some really important issue of foreign affairs he would bring out a thoroughly human and enlightening detail which he had learnt and stored away somewhere.

I have been disappointed by what people have written about Ernie. Alan Bullock's *Life of Ernest Bevin* was quite fascinating, a full and splendid record of most of Ernie's marvellous career. But it is so full of facts, and complicated facts at that, that it is very difficult really to see what sort of man Ernie was. Bullock's book, though good, does not make Ernie come alive. Other people seem to have confined themselves to telling funny stories about him, or praising him in general ways without really going into what made him tick. I have never liked this either, but, being not much good as a Private Secretary, I was never so much involved in his work as was Bob Dixon or Nicko Henderson who were much more in the political fray all the time.

I think one of the things that makes for a good diplomat is curiosity, trying to find out why things happen and see therefore why they may happen again or something else may happen next time. Ernie was immensely curious because he was also tremendously interested. He looked at the world with the eyes almost of innocence, with a wonder about how things happened, how the country at which he was looking survived and prospered. This was particularly true of the United States, where he had seen a polyglot and varied section of humanity swarming ashore and somehow forming themselves into a great nation.

I have never met any other politician, or, indeed, person, who was either anything like so interested or so well-informed about how foreign people tick, work, and look at others outside their boundaries. It was curious how he easily he got onto the wavelength of some of the Ambassadors who came from unfamiliar parts of the world, such as Sidky Pasha, the outstanding Egyptian politician of his generation. For some reason Ernie tended to take to Ambassadors from rather obscure countries. He was very fond of the Guatemalan Ambassador, and Mrs. Bevin was very keen on the Iraqi Ambassador. Though quick witted, one had to play to his strengths. He could understand a point very quickly, but liked to have papers very simply phrased, particularly the first paragraph. He might or might not read the supplementary information, but he would always grasp the essence. Ernie was the archetype for those who want to be ministers. He also possessed extraordinary integrity: Mrs. Bevin never used the official car for any private purpose because it might look corrupt.

Ernie never had the faintest feeling of inferiority with people who had had every advantage, whereas he had, before he grew up, so few opportunities. There were, however, no, or very few, prejudices or chips on his ample shoulders and he was always able to deal with the greatest experts in all sorts of subjects without being in any way over-awed or feeling slighted by them. He had, even in the face of great displays of learning, an original view of his own which made a contribution and was usually culled from his own observations of life. It was also remarkable that he should reach the level he did without any advantages. His mother died when he was six, and he had no formal education at all.

He was, I believe, a marvellous man, and we in this country have very much missed him, more than we realise, since he died. He had no time for the cheap or meretricious. There were some subjects, such as the Trades Disputes Act which he fought for and felt passionate about but he was never unfair or underhand. Some thought he bulldozed his way through opposition, but I always remember going to Conferences with him when he had been away and there had been rebellious grumblings. He did not win by bulldozing his enemies; he won because he convinced them. That was largely because he was himself convinced and his sincerity showed through and won the day. And at the crunch he always seemed to stand above faction and party prejudice and to care for the interests of all the people. That was a great strength, though he was not always merciful to those he thought cheaply demagogic, partisan, or dishonest.

I have never much liked the anecdotal approach to Ernest Bevin. The anecdotes are sometimes very valuable in illustrating how he worked and the pithy way he had of summarising some important lesson he had learnt in life in two or three words. Yet I always feel that some of this story-telling has a rather patronising, condescending air about it, particularly from some diplomatic sources where one almost feels that it is an attempt to show how the Foreign Office, which really did value him, tamed and domesticated this unusual phenomenon, who came from a very different background from that of themselves. Gladwyn Jebb always called him "Uncle Ernie", for instance, and Derick Hoyer-Millar always spoke to Ernie as if they were in a meeting, which Ernie hated. First reactions of opponents tended to be that he was sort of an illiterate lout, because he tended to drop his "h's" or was never much of an orator even at his best.

He had a naturally marvellous and spontaneous brain, which would go on working efficiently through dreary, exhausting negotiations. He always had a sharp eye for what was happening around him and a very great imagination for what might start happening next. He said to me after one meeting with Gladwyn Jebb: "I enjoyed that, Henniker. I like Gladwyn, you know. His mind's always moving, always makes you move too. And 'e 'as 100 ideas; 99 of them are balls, but one of them is bloody good. He never knows which one, though."

Ernie also had one characteristic I have only seen to so marked an extent in him and in no-one else I have met in life. He could not easily give up a lost cause. If he ran into a brick wall, such as Palestine, he immediately picked himself up and started planning how to get round, under, or over, the wall. He did not bash his head against it uselessly, but really thought that there was some way he could get to the other side and get others to join him there. It is I think said to be the greatest characteristic of great generals to be able to do this because they so often in a military disaster seem to be at a dead end. Ernie possessed this quality to an extraordinary extent. He was always constructive under all circumstances and went on against every possible discouragement and opposition, often almost total from the Russians for example, in trying to find a way to mutual understanding. He was always thinking of a problem in terms of a solution. Ernie was incredibly hard-working; a model in this respect.

There were only a very few times when he proved to be less than a great success. This was, I think, mainly in the Middle East, and was often due to the fact that his health was never quite good enough. Some of the things he did would have had much better results if he could have done them personally, but his health would not allow him to go to places like Cairo and Baghdad, where his personal presence would, I think, have done what others could not achieve without him.

Ernie's health was not a concern confined to his last months. His Egyptian plans were thwarted because he could not travel to Cairo to meet Sidky Pasha, with whom he had conducted a detailed correspondence. Our relations with the Egyptians would have been improved to the point that the Suez crisis would have been unlikely. The same was true for Baghdad. He declined clearly during my time with him, particularly in cold climates, where we really had to be very careful to keep him warm. Even in 1946 as I wrote to Os, less than a year into Ernie's tenure as Foreign Secretary: "Today we had the Secretary of State back again for the first time and the usual scamper started all over again. He seems much better, but still a little low. He's really been quite ill. We should have forced him to get away after the last conference, but somehow couldn't quite do it. There was always something he had to be about for. I was with him in the House when he started to feel ill and was really rather worried." There was a consistent decline in his health, but he would never trade on it. I knew his doctor quite well, and he would tell me how at the end of his day when Ernie got home, Mrs. Bevin would have him pushing furniture around all night, re-arranging the house. He kept long hours, and the poor fellow could hardly breathe.

I wept when I heard that he had died. It was not a surprise, however. My immediate reaction was that we would never know his like again. If, luckily, a new Ernest Bevin were born someone would get hold of him and send him to some fine educational institution and educate his spontaneity out of him and make him conform to fashionable intellectual views. When I left the Private Office he said, "Henniker, I've always appreciated you being so straight with me". I was mildly surprised that he might think I would be anything but straight with him. He was one of the really great men in the whole spectrum of our political life and somehow people should remember how great he was. He remains without parallel in my experience.

NINE

Os, *1948 to 1960*

My period in the Private Office was marked by extremes of fulfilment and frustration. I wrote home from Moscow in 1946: "I didn't realise that being a temporary bachelor again would seem so nasty and squalid, drinking and gossiping and messing about deep into the night". The problem, I soon realised, was that I missed Os.

Before I came back from Belgrade, Ralph Stevenson said I must meet some girls and think about marriage. I had no such matters in my mind. I was very innocent in those days. In Yugoslavia we lived a chaste life of rectitude. I never slept with a girl all the time I was a partisan. There was no way to let off steam. Aware of this Ralph said there was someone whose mother he knew, Osla Benning, a Canadian, who was not only beautiful but also clever. He introduced us in London at a party at the Savoy. I was deeply disappointed. I expected a little Dresden shepherdess or blond *bergère*; there she was, dark-hair flying in all directions. She was a semi-diplomat working in the Conference department, which dealt mainly with delegations and were in control of administration. She was very different from what I expected, and though I was not immediately taken with her, we met again and eventually hit it off. She was full of pep and vim and was the sort of girl who always knew the head waiter. Before long we were going out together.

Os was a very precious and lovely person who throughout her life had felt a bit excluded. She had been born in Canada; her father was a rich American, thanks to the Canadian Pacific Railway, and her mother a rich Canadian. Her parents' marriage broke up almost immediately and Os was always brought up by her mother, who was fond of her but pretty useless as

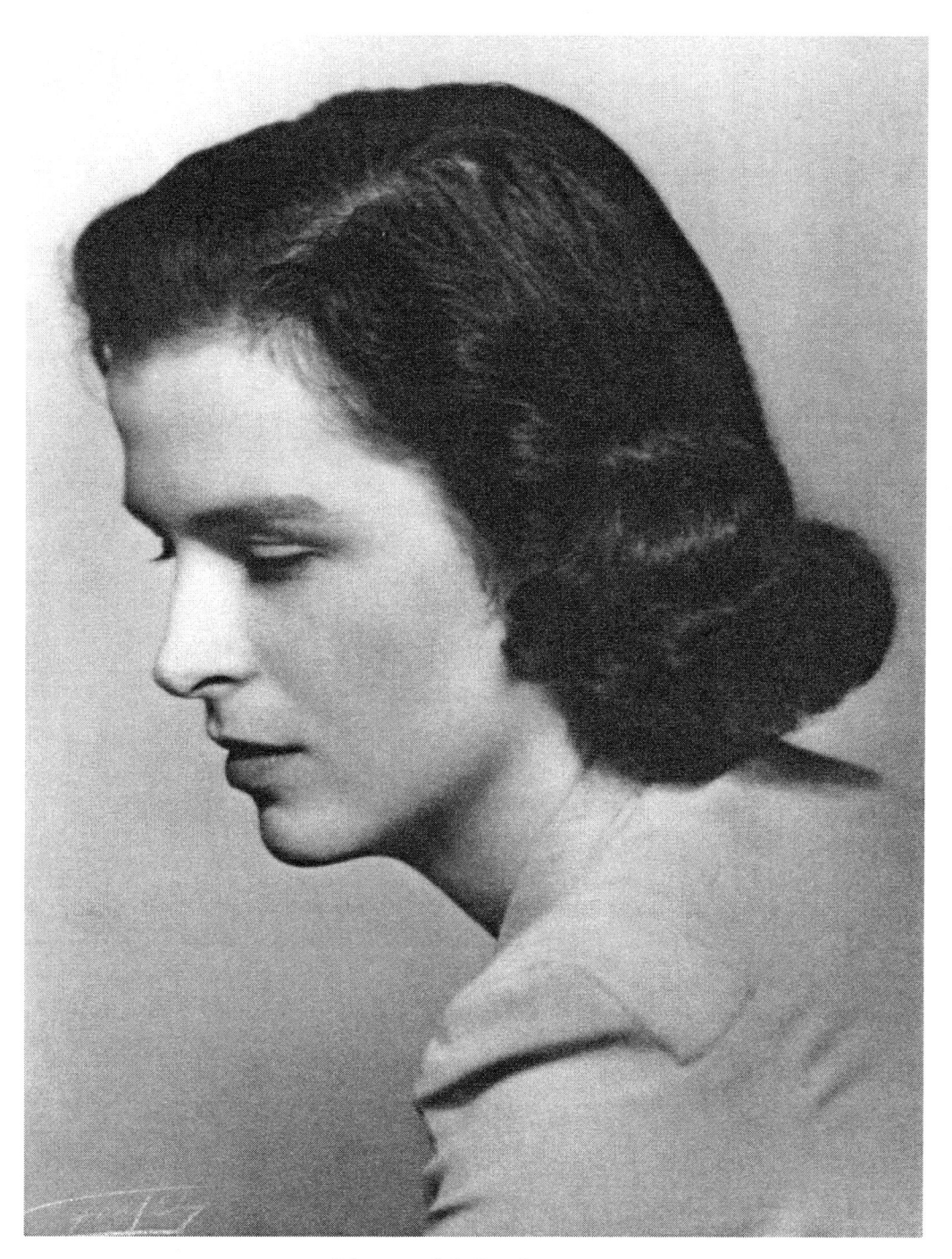

Margaret Osla Benning, 1947.

a mother; Os was always left with nanny in the country. We were told by her mother that Os' father was little more than a drunk, but later discovered that we had received a very slanted account.

From the outset, I feared Os was far too sophisticated for me. She was known to be friends with Prince Philip and at every restaurant we went to, she seemed to have a corner table. Then, slowly, I came to realise, that she was a very straightforward simple girl. Her friendship with Prince Philip was innocent, but Philip was told by his Uncle, Lord Mountbatten, to go to Australia to join the navy and soon afterwards he became engaged to Princess Elizabeth.

Before the engagement was announced in 1947, Anthony Strachey invited Os and me to dine with the Princesses Elizabeth and Margaret. His intention was that Os could tell the future Queen about Philip. I know Philip thought I was not quite good enough for Os, but he appeared to reform his opinion and he told a friend years later, "I now see what she saw in him!"

Osla's friendship with Prince Philip made it a little difficult with the press, which was always digging away to find some relationship between them, there was nothing to find.

In contrast to me, Os was very popular and was in fact much in demand socially. She was very pretty, with a lovely lively personality. She did cast a spell, it was quite disconcerting within the Foreign Office because all the men who were not homosexual thought they were in love with her.

I proposed to Os in Paris while we were there at the Peace Conference. She accepted. I was frightfully bad for a bit, not writing, and so on. She was full of tears and thought I had forgotten about her. While I was in Moscow I began to miss her dreadfully. We would speak on the telephone and she would burst into tears. I declined to go to New York with Ernie, and stayed behind to get married on 18th December 1946.

Os was an angel who walked into my life. Brave, tireless in helping others and ready to take on anybody who was in difficulties. My parents took to Os, and father regarded her as a bird of paradise, which had misguidedly strayed into my cage. Nothing could have been happier than our marriage and looking back on it I can only count my blessings.

TEN

The Foreign Office, 1938 to 1968

In 1948 my time came to move on from the Private Office. I was asked what I next wanted to do, and said that I wanted to become an economist. The Foreign Office is a curious place in that no one is ever taught anything. One arrives, is put somewhere, and then expected to get on with it.

People with an aptitude for economics were brought into Mutual Aid department, which was dealing with the Marshall Plan and expected to learn on the job. I did not know much about Mutual Aid or the Marshall Plan, and did not know much about economics; nor did I learn much. The start of Mutual Aid convinced me that I needed to know more. In the Foreign Office there was a tremendous dominant opinion that the only worthwhile speciality was political. More and more however, it became clear that the economic side was growing in significance, and that we were seriously lacking qualified staff.

I was posted to serve as Assistant Head (First Secretary) of the European Recovery department, created to deal with Mutual Aid under Paul Gore-Booth. I had had a very close relationship with Hall-Patch who had, as Deputy Under-Secretary, taken over as Senior Economist in the Foreign Office. We saw a lot of each other because, both being conscientious we would be at work at the weekend when there were few others there. When Gore-Booth moved on I took over.

Mutual Aid had been another of Ernie's achievements. I was there for about two years and was mainly under the control of the Treasury. The Foreign Office did not have much to do with it: we were not the prime movers because we had not enough economists. I did not like my time there much as I never knew what was happening, largely because matters were out of my hands. It was difficult because the Treasury tended to control matters, and when I was invited to attend meetings I did not understand what was being discussed and seldom had a contribution to make. I spent most of my time writing papers, which I did not understand, to Roger Makins, Head of Economics, who did not understand them either. When I was promoted to Head of Personnel, little in this area in the Foreign Office had changed. My time there did at least provide an awareness of the problems with which other departments were having to deal. It was also very useful in that through it I met many people in the service I would not otherwise have met. The experience served to provide the seed for a policy which took root when I returned to Whitehall.

One day I was called in to the Personnel department, and was told that there was a vacancy as Head of Chancery in Buenos Aires. I accepted, despite knowing absolutely nothing about Argentina. As usually happens in the Foreign Office I was, within a week, the Embassy's expert. I was successful in Buenos Aires, and enjoyed it enormously, mainly because I was always very busy, but also, perhaps, because it was a vast country full of beautiful women and a country life which I knew from England. I liked the city very much, as well as the country.

Osla and I quickly realised that we were both pretty good at diplomatic life, loved each other deeply, had started and were pleased with our little family, and were eager for a new challenge. Our flat in Buenos Aires was hideous, but constantly full of people. I had, I hope, a good reputation amongst the Argentines whom, despite our reputed quarrels with them, we usually liked very much.

We had many friends. We entertained and danced and went out a lot. I had a nice lot of work to do as Head of Chancery, which I much enjoyed because it gave me a chance to put my finger in every pie and to be responsible for administering a large staff which involved many nice Anglo-Argentines and a pretty good British staff.

I had gone out there without any clear understanding of what I was to do. The most significant recent development had been the nationalisation of most British enterprises by the Argentine government. I found that my predecessor had spent all his time trying to resolve the question of pensions without any success whatsoever. When the railways were nationalised, many British employees were made redundant, and the Embassy was trying to get pensions for them. My predecessor used to go regularly to the Ministry of Foreign Affairs to talk about this. He said the Argentines were impossible to deal with.

I tested the ground as soon as I arrived, and found no sign of hostility; the Argentines seemed very friendly and willing. They had no idea what my predecessor had been talking about. I got down to brass tacks, and went off to the Ministry of Transport and sat in a queue of visitors. I continued to wait in the Minister's ante-room for days, having made various appointments, none of which were kept. I asked an Englishman who happened to be waiting with me "is this where a proper Englishman rises to his feet and marches out?" "I don't know," said the man, who happened to be a railwayman, "I've been coming here six days myself". I waited.

The Minister of Transport when I finally got to see him, and not knowing why I was there, gave me a car and an escort to see all the offices where they were dealing with pensions. We wandered off down the byways of Buenos Aires where minor government offices were situated and where they had never seen an Englishman before. We went from scruffy office to scruffy office, everyone was splendidly polite and thrilled to see us.

It took me about two years before any results could be seen and at the end of my time I had a settlement of every claim. Even those who had gone off to places like Bolivia, to work on the railways there, got pensions. I thought we had done a good job. It was probably the most successful thing I have ever done as a diplomat: I had started it, and got the whole problem cleared up. It was a good example of how an Embassy can take up and resolve the problems of British subjects abroad.

The pensions matter took up most of my time, but in so doing I got to know most of the people in Buenos Aires who mattered, and when I was not shooting with the Italian Ambassador, I played golf with a fellow from the Ministry of Foreign Affairs, and he usually beat me, which helped. I managed to learn Spanish in a week. All the younger staff, and Jock Balfour, who was hopeless, were taught to dance the rumba, cha cha and samba in the Embassy to the agonised cries of Lady Balfour to the Ambassador, "This isn't a waltz it is a samba, and you're treading on my toes".

It was a happy and cheerful Embassy. A very nice and talented junior secretary joined us – Mervyn Brown, who distinguished himself in almost every field of activity. He had succeeded a rather less attractive secretary, Leslie Minford, who was quite taken with Foreign Office privileges, especially the drink. We had a top class archivist in Harry Rogers, whom I hope got promotion later, and some excellent secretaries. There was also a group of "friends" – semi-spies – whose activities at that time were well known and were not very useful. They were replaced by a very useful Intelligence Officer, Paul Matthews, son-in-law of a senior Mexican diplomat who was invariably informed of Argentine secrets, particularly those of their navy. It was sad that his successor should have been summarily disposed of by Mrs. Thatcher and not replaced, for any replacement would automatically have been fully informed before the Argentine navy took steps against the Falklands.

We had two Ambassadors in my time; one good, one less so. Jock Balfour, our first was very nice. As a student he had been interned in Germany during the First World War. A very emotional man and occasionally theatrical, he was always making inappropriate great speeches in the Ministry of Foreign Affairs about meat or the pensions. He thought they would have enormous effect, but they seldom did. He never had any real contact with the Argentines, and did not find them congenial. Both he and his charming wife Frances were longing to move, and to their joy eventually went to Spain. He always thought that he knew everything, while I was frightfully cautious. He said, "John, you look like a Dago but you're nothing like as clever as any of them".

Our next Ambassador was less exciting: Sir Henry Bradshaw Mack. He had come from Baghdad where everything had blown up around him, and where he had done little to understand or warn us about a catastrophic revolution when the King was murdered. He had a good Embassy though, in Buenos Aires, and quite liked me. It helped that he could not stand his official number two, the Counsellor, who would be sent off to funeral services for which he was usually late and wearing the wrong clothes. Sir Henry, however, was very lazy. He and his Irish wife never seemed to have learnt anything about diplomacy in all their long careers.

The Falklands War in 1982 marred previously excellent relations, which was one of the reasons Mrs. Thatcher's embrace of war was so unfortunate, particularly given that but for the lack of one patrol vessel in the South

Atlantic the invasion would probably never have happened. There had been a great admiration for things British, and a long connection with Britain. We had seen them through independence, and whenever they could they would try to acquire the appurtenances of British life, such as membership of a smart club. Their country life was an idealised form of ours, with shooting, and polo everywhere. A great many of their naval officers had been through Dartmouth. While I was there, there was never any murmur of territorial or any other disagreements. There were often grouses about Britain's acquisition of the Malvinas, with some reason, as its early history was a fairly sordid story on our part. I did write a paper mentioning the need to look properly at the problem.

Peron's government was poor, corrupt and usually rabble rousing and strongly nationalistic, particularly where his wife Evita was concerned. He was little more than a buccaneering local bully-boy, with a tendency to look favourably on communists or anyone else hostile to the West. He embraced the paradox of a statesman who was not especially biddable but who was also all things to all men. There was a secret police, and though many people were put in prison, they were not badly treated by the standards of South America. It was all much harsher under the following regime, which took over three years after I had left. It was all very messy. We heard about the various intrigues taking place, usually amongst the military entourage around Peron. Peron and Evita were generally hostile to us, because of their close relationship with the Nazis. In fact, I had a visceral dislike of the Peron regime, just as I did when I had seen Hitler in Germany.

Most of the Peronists were corrupt, and propaganda was very prevalent. Nevertheless, the government was not adept at presenting an attractive picture of the country or of themselves to the international community. The nationalisation of the railways had not endeared them to the regime in London, which had invested so heavily in it originally.

Peron's charisma was obvious, and the great rallies were undoubtedly impressive. On 26th July 1952 we were going to have a farewell party on the night before we left for London at the end of our posting. In the house next door to ours, Evita was dying. She had cancer, and was only 33. Since she died that night, at 9.42, the party had to be cancelled. We left the next morning under something of a dark cloud.

ELEVEN

Personnel, 1953 to 1960

With heavy heart Osla and I had left the Argentine and come back to England. On a very small income we had a nice flat in Knightsbridge with two maids. I was told by some of the people in the know that I ought to get a good job next because I had been sent to what was reckoned in the Foreign Office as outer darkness in Argentina, which I had found totally blissful, playing golf, tennis and dancing all night and including a Fleet visit from the West Indies Station. I had no idea what sort of post I was hoping for or what I wanted to do. The general consensus in the Private Office was that I had been rather badly treated to be sent to South America. There were various suggestions: I could go to Paris if Bob Dixon wanted me to or to the United Nations in New York as number two. Tony Rumbold, who was senior to me, decided to go himself to New York, and so I remained in London. I was actually very glad. I did not want to go to New York. My mother-in-law lived there.

Someone thought of Bonn, which I did not want. Then one day I went to lunch with my old boss Ashley Clarke, who was off to be Ambassador in Rome. I told Ashley, who had been my boss in the Far Eastern department, that I would prefer to go back to Yugoslavia or some more distant post. After a few formal preliminaries he said, "John I'm going to offer you something which most of your colleagues would regard as the kiss of death and I expect you to turn it down. Robin Hooper is leaving the Personnel department and we need someone to replace him as its head." It was, he said a tricky and particularly worrying job, after the recent and sudden departure of Burgess and Maclean to the Soviet Union and the whole thing had been a particular trial to Robin. The incident would be bound to have a lot of repercussions and would need a firm hand and a totally new security set-up with measures to avoid repetition. He said I'd end up with no friends at all as everyone would think that I ought to advance their career and I would neither want nor be able to do so.

I had never thought of such a job, but I realised as soon as Ashley spoke, that bells rang in my mind – it was exactly what I wanted to do. I don't know why; I loved people, lots of them, and the more difficult the better. I was desperately proud to have got into the Diplomatic Service and thought that I might be able, without ruffling too many feathers, to make it an even better career for diplomats than it looked at present. "I'd love to do it and the sooner the better while the wounds of the spies are still there." I realised that Ashley was in effect also saying to me that the Service needed pulling together to take on the responsibility given to it by the report written by Bevin and Eden after the war. This report sorted out most of the problems of different pay scales and brought together a service which could, in effect, be called on to serve whenever or wherever the Secretary of State wished, abroad or in Whitehall. I was to have a pretty free hand. No one ever tried to give me any advice. Ashley agreed with me that I should take over as soon as Robin Hooper was found a suitable post.

I moved up into the Personnel department, taking over from Hooper as its Head about a year later. I was there for more than 10 years, and never regretted my decision. The clout and prestige of the Personnel department at that stage had never been high. The Service élite always saw it as a slightly menial, rather unpleasant job, and it was offered to me in those terms; as a necessary but nuts and bolts sort of doctor's job which no diplomat could or should really expect to enjoy. When I arrived I indeed found the department still shaken and slightly bogged-down in all the aftermath of the Burgess and Maclean disappearances. I had not been surprised, but a lot of people at the Foreign Office were quite dumbfounded. The Service was built on the belief that we were all gentlemen and it came as a dreadful shock than any alleged gentleman – especially one with the impeccable credentials of Maclean – could do what he had done. Burgess was less of a shock. And was known to be an unreliable bad hat.

When I was offered Personnel, in the midst of the gloom in the Foreign Office, I was, however, quite delighted – to the surprise of everyone. I had always been attracted by it, and I was pleased with the recent Eden-Bevin reforms. One of the things that specially interested me was that there seemed to be a chance of really doing something and because I have always found people much more interesting than anything else, this natural empathy now had a suitable outlet.

I had often talked to colleagues in the Foreign Office and when I was abroad in Belgrade, about the excitement that the career was offering and the improved conditions and pay, but they often seemed resigned that there was no chance of changing the arbitrary system of promotion that seemed to exist.

With the recent experience I had had of Henry Mack in Buenos Aries, I was determined that there would be changes. The Service had to be cleaned up and with so many people back from the war, all at about the same rank, it was very cluttered up, though the Sir Somebody Somethings who littered Whitehall were dying off.

While I had been in Belgrade, the Foreign Service had been amalgamated with the Diplomatic Service, but there was little feeling of liberation for the people in the combined service, which depressed me. It should have meant that appointments were made on the basis of merit, not length of service, and that those at even the lower reaches, could now reach the top. This also went for women, and Bevin I knew, was particularly keen that there should be free movement of people according to merit climbing the ladder up the Service.

I took a great personal interest in all postings, trying to see that the Service used and rewarded special qualities, and that this should start at the beginning of a diplomat's career in a structure that would make them more useful as they climbed the pyramid of promotion. I wanted to get rid of a conveyor belt mentality.

From the moment that Ashley Clarke recommended me to take on a special role in the Personnel department, I was assimilated into the Promotions Board which met regularly under the Chairman, the PUS – Derick Hoyer-Millar and had, as members, all the Under-Secretaries in the Foreign Office.

There was a curious feeling that it was quite improper for members of the Promotions Board to interfere with the agendas which it was my responsibility to prepare, or to suggest ways of solving the problems of the postings of which we were faced.

To this end I was fairly outspoken at meetings in order to hasten and modernise the process: I tried to induce the Board to see this as a joint operation in which I was merely supplying the background information while they suggested the solutions.

This was a conscious effort to re-calibrate the Foreign Office mindset after the war and the end of Empire, to deal with new realities, and Britain's place in the world. This did not mean that it was widely recognised and certainly not widely appreciated. It took a long period of total disbelief to change our self-perception. Britain now, for example, had to go out in the world and tout for business. There was a need to shake up what often came near to complacency, and as Head of Personnel, I was given some means of effecting these changes.

Trade had become increasingly important and provided a new ladder of promotion as Britain learnt to sell its goods abroad.

By the early fifties the physical changes of incorporating into a unified Service, all the separate Services, such as the Levant, China, Japan, and Siam Consular Services, as well as the Commercial Diplomatic Service, had been more or less achieved, though the consequences of this had not been assimilated into the thinking and practices of the Service. The most obviously worrying of these when I arrived was that a large number of people in the China Consular Service who had been trained only in Chinese had, after the communist victory, nowhere to go, and one had to scratch around everywhere to find places (usually unsuitable) in which to put them. At the same time the India, Pakistan and Sudan and Colonial Services were either needing us or about to need us to harbour some of their staff and the older hands had got used to being stuck in a backwater and had lost much of whatever ambition they had had. In the Consular Service people tended to get buried and lost unless, as was the case with Colin Crowe and Denis Wright, they were unusually good and distinguished themselves.

I think it was at this time when I was dealing with the Board of Trade over improving our commercial knowledge, that the idea of jazzing up MECAS – the Middle East Centre of Arab Studies – took shape, out of talks I had with Donald Maitland. I cannot remember quite why he became a close confidante of mine at that time, perhaps originally because my wife and his sister-in-law were both Canadians; perhaps it was because when I worked with Ernie we were much involved in Middle Eastern questions and Donald was often at our elbow.

I think people always find it hard to credit that there was almost, until I left the Personnel department, nothing even remotely resembling a central planning unit or forum in which plans for people's careers, however primitive, could be made or at least discussed. Policies emerged from interplay between the officials who happened to know the most about any important candidate or subject which came up, and where the key jobs were likely to be. And also, who were in the best placed jobs, usually heads of departments. One example was Martin Le Quesne, who was almost unchallenged in the influence he exercised over such policy as the Foreign Office had for Africa. Ernie Bevin really tried and was indefatigably ingenious in getting things really right and in not just trying to look like a boss, as did Morrison and others. Occasionally other sources of influence – energetic and interested Ambassadors – played a part, though it was strange how few diplomats were really interested in Foreign Affairs. From the beginning of my time in the Personnel department I was aware of and troubled by the curious lacuna of the total lack of any planning mechanism or body which could express a coherent view on British foreign policy. This often left us oddly weak in a crisis or in arguing with other government departments. On, I think, three occasions, I tried to set one up, but the opposition was determined. Sometimes it was covert, and opposed mainly on the grounds that people had more than enough to do and did not want to take on another function; sometimes more overt. I remember Adam Watson fiercely opposing a Planning Unit. I had suggested the Horn of Africa as a good place to start planning how we might achieve our real interests. He said that it would merely provoke a lot of nugatory work and that, if any part of the world was important and interesting, it would equally interest other powers whose main aim would be to frustrate the achievement of our aims. I argued that it would, at least, be valuable to know what our real interests were so that if there were any let-up in the constant struggle he envisaged, we could then set about trying to realise them rather than reacting to the situation by drifting aimlessly while we tried to decide what to do, as has happened so often as the pace and development of Foreign Affairs speeded up.

Much had to change as a result of The Spies. Burgess and Maclean had the effect of shattering the entire culture of the Foreign Office. It appeared that men who had been at the centre of events and with apparently impeccable

left:
Janey, Charly and Mark at Petleys Downe, 1957.

below:
Mark, Osla, Janey and Charly at Petleys Downe, 1959.

backgrounds and believed to be gentlemen were totally unreliable. It was a complete shock to the department and the Foreign Office itself. Many people were amazed but I, who am naturally fairly sceptical about people I know, found it hard to be really surprised. People are weak and do change and it helped of course that I had heard rumours about Maclean and knew more about Burgess from Cambridge. What really surprised me was that Nicko Henderson, who was a close friend of mine and who had worked with Donald Maclean in Washington and shared a flat with him, seemed unable to believe or grasp what had happened. It was obvious to me, even at this early stage, that a lot had to be done and there might well even be some opposition to imposing more restrictions on the staff. Strangely enough, much of the talk was very much as it was after the destruction of the twin towers in New York. The world, they said, would never be quite the same again.

We had to get down to examining what had happened and how to prevent it happening again and looking at the possibility of new security rules being applied. We were speedily given small additions to the staff which enabled us to examine with greater care the background and activities of our staff. It was, for example, well known that Maclean had shown traces of suspicious and unusual behaviour in London and gone around saying to everyone he knew that "they" were after him. No one had taken any notice. New security rules were introduced as quickly as possible, but it was regarded at the same time as very important not to shake the whole ship and spread the seeds of distrust, which, for the first time, hit the Foreign Office. These were the first steps needed to start a new and more rigorous system of working, choosing and vetting staff.

The main theme of my first period in Personnel was, I felt, to demystify it. A sort of belief had spread through the Service that Personnel had extraordinary rules about promoting or blocking the progress of people they didn't approve of, and very long memories of any failing shown at any stage in a career. I think I convinced most people of the honesty of the department, of its readiness to discuss their hopes and fears about their careers and to reassure them either that all was well or that they would have to pull their socks up in various ways before they could hope for promotion. The rules, in fact, were almost exactly as they would be in any normal undertaking. I was shocked when I eventually went to the British

Council to find that any failings committed a decade ago were produced as confirmation that someone was unsuitable for some post that they quite legitimately hoped for and were aiming at.

To get a new Service working properly one had to gain its friendship and confidence. At the top I found it easy. Our new Permanent Under-Secretary was Derick Hoyer-Millar, in whom I and I think most of his colleagues, had complete confidence. He might not have been the cleverest man in the Service but there were no doubts anywhere that he had every quality required to ensure that people were promoted as far as possible on the basis of their performance. It is true to say that under Derick Hoyer-Millar, the Service quickly came to be seen as fair, open and working on common sense lines. In short, we all felt that we were very lucky to belong to a Service that was so well run and fairly operated. The rest of the senior staff really took the same line as he did. I also managed to collect round me a staff which came from many different stables and would attract and keep the confidence of the Service. New recruits were trusted and treated with confidence as soon as they were properly known and had shown their capacity. I had at my elbow and as my confidants people as different as a Wykamist, at least two products from comprehensive schools, a young army officer and a rather dissident socialist Etonian. Indeed we tried to choose people who could understand and treat with confidence most of the people who were now entering the Service. If they fitted with our needs they were given further training, and only if they did not reach the standard we were looking for were they eventually moved to less testing stations.

We worked in perfect harmony and everyone was expected to take full responsibility for the people they managed. I was always pretty well informed about what was happening anyway, for it has always been my practice to believe that one never hears the truth unless one shows one completely trusts one's staff. It is, of course, hard to remain popular in a job like that, but I think I was seen to be fair and I learnt very quickly that one must never be seen to be influenced by anything but the professional ability of the candidate and the needs of the Service. I felt as long as I was there I must avoid over-promoting those I liked and especially approved of. Indeed the one thing one has to remember is that no promotion or demotion must be designed to give one personal pleasure unless it is obviously deserved and the word "me" must be expunged from the vocabulary of any personnel officer.

A central part of the job was inspecting staff around the world. I did a tour of the Middle East, and then the Far East checking that people were happy and in the right places. They may be unhappy thinking that the Ivory Coast was the end of the earth, but with a word of encouragement and a pat on the back they could be reassured. I knew from my own experience of being abroad and being alone how much personal considerations could affect the ability of a diplomat to function effectively. The tours were very useful, and I got to know people much better. It was certainly preferable to sitting behind a desk in London.

Another innovation I attempted was in trying to be as open as I could. The Foreign Office has always been shrouded in secrecy. There is a need for some secrecy, of course, but it had become in some cases, secrecy to the point of mumbo-jumbo. I used to try and discuss with people what they thought their future was, and what they wanted to do. Through acting with kindness many things which would otherwise have been extremely unpleasant could be achieved. People could not be sacked, so much as shuffled off. I had to send someone from Casablanca to Shanghai, and I asked him to see me. He told me he hated China. I told him that was all there was. He was Rhodesian, and mentioned that if Mozambique was available he would like that. I remembered this, and when a post in Maputo came up, I got back in touch with him. He wired back that he did not actually want to go to Mozambique, but merely would rather have gone there than to Shanghai. Sometimes a Head of Personnel cannot win.

After the communist revolution we had to wind down the China Service because Mao Tze Tung kept closing down the consulates, and so we had to find jobs for surplus China specialists. One hoped it would work but occasionally it didn't and then they had to be specially found a job that might actually suit them. We found posts for most of them. When we had to find places for members of the Sudan Service which we took over piecemeal and which was a very specialist Service, and the Colonial Service, as they gradually became our business while the Empire shrank. We found suitable jobs for everyone; even and including the only judge in the Sudan Service and I think they were all reasonably happy.

Loneliness and boredom were the main problems for overseas staff. We also had some trouble with Ambassadors and their fondness for drink or women; or men. In the event of rumours that the garden path was full of drink bottles, or that the Ambassador had been caught in bed with the Peruvian Under-Secretary, I would send out a special inspection team to have a look. We had an Ambassador in San Salvador who had cats; hundreds of them. The Embassy stank of cat pee and we had to move him on. The Service could be rather uncoordinated. One chap in Tokyo went to the dentist and disappeared. One day a telegram came in from the Embassy in Nicaragua. "We have your counsellor. What shall we do with him?" One Ambassador I had to try and get divorced from his wife because she jumped into bed with everybody in public. I wrote to him to tell him, and he did eventually decide that it would be best to get a divorce rather than have constant rows with the Service.

My impression at the end of my time was that we had a pretty good and well equipped Service capable of doing all that was asked of it. There were still important things to be tackled and I hoped, when I went later to the British Council, that I could still play a part in reform, but that was denied me for reasons I will explain later. I was sad about this but it was, I think, just fate and perhaps I overestimated what I thought I would be able to do.

There was one other development which is worth mentioning; when I was in the Far Eastern department of the Foreign Office, Sir John Pratt, brother of Boris Karloff, had been Consul General in Shanghai, and had suddenly started to change his colour. He got blacker, and ended up looking like Krishna Menon. In those days the British colony were pretty conservative and agitated strongly for him to be removed. He was brought back to London and when he arrived he came naturally to the Far Eastern department where his friends were likely to be. There had been two young secretaries in that department; myself and Tom Bromley, a young Japan Consul. I think that Pratt hoped that his daughter Diana might marry one of us. She did marry Tom. At that time there was no machinery to look after the urgent human problems that came up in Personnel. Tom had been posted to Washington and while there his wife was following in her father's footsteps: she was changing colour. She had a very bad time, pushed off sidewalks and sworn at as being black. She returned to Britain in a bad state, and had a severe nervous breakdown. With Cornelius Medvei a great supporter and friend and the Treasury medical adviser – we put her into hospital several times, but owing to the law, could not keep her there against her will. I was very worried about her, and kept in constant touch with Medvei who was an enormous help. We knew how concerned she was about the future of her two boys and I consulted Medvei about the likelihood of her committing suicide, which he most feared. However hard one tried it was impossible to guard against such an event. One night, just before Christmas, Tom called to say he had come home and could not find his wife. There were signs of a struggle in the house, and in the end she was found in a state of collapse next to her two sons who had been murdered. Tom, who was immensely brave, refused my offer of a bed that night after the police had found the children.

We realised that there must have been something more we could have done and as soon as the Bromley case had been tried and Diana sentenced to Broadmoor for life, we set up an organisation called Diplomatic Wives on the lines already pioneered with the Commonwealth Office which had had the same sort of experiences. It was headed by Mrs. Anthony Elliot the wife of one of my assistants in the Personnel department, and it remained in place until after I had been posted abroad when it was presided over by Lady Williams, the wife of our Ambassador in Spain. I am very happy to see that a new dispensation has been made for wives in a similar situation and I hope it will continue: it is very necessary in a Service such as ours.

Tom was a brave man and emerged from his tragedy with his sanity intact. He tried to go on visiting Diana in Broadmoor but we were able in the end to persuade him that she no longer even knew who he was and that life had to go on being lived. We offered him a post in Somalia, which was then more hopeful and productive than it has recently been, and he agreed to go Mogadishu, accompanied by a friend from the administrative side of the Foreign Office; Frank Sargeant, with whom he was very close. I gave Frank specific instructions not to let Tom out of his sight. I think Tom enjoyed Somalia and eventually happily married the widow of an Oxford don and went with her as the last British Ambassador in Addis Abbaba in the reign of Haile Selassie. There he served alongside my very able number two Willie Morris, who had been with me in Jordan, and his very attractive American wife Ghislaine who wrote to me after the Emperor was deposed and imprisoned with agonised accounts of his dreadful treatment and that of his family, many of whom were murdered by the revolutionaries who had formed the Deng government.

The real test came in 1956 when I was left holding the baby over the invasion of Egypt. I was involved in the Suez disaster from an early stage, and regard my role of averting mutiny and preventing a wholesale resignation of staff as being one of the most useful contributions I made during my time at the Foreign Office.

One day urgent telegrams suddenly started coming in. We heard from the Israelis that we, with them, were attacking Egypt. It became very plain to me almost immediately that I had a particularly ghastly problem on my hands. The spirit of rebellion was running very high amongst our staff in the Middle East. People were dismayed. Humphrey Trevelyan had just arrived as Ambassador and without even warning him Eden suddenly gave orders to attack Cairo, announcing that Britain could not allow Nasser to take over the running of the Canal as he had done, and we were therefore sending troops into Egypt.

Everyone I knew was furious. It was very disheartening for the Service, and naturally enough people came to me to express their dismay. A clear majority was appalled by what the government was doing. I said I would do my best to tell a reasonably high quarter how feelings in the Service were running. I had thought a little bit about what I would do if an emergency occurred, and I spoke to Eddie Playfair, an important Under-Secretary in the Treasury who was very well informed about the Middle East and the natural duties of government in such a crisis. He told me that it was absolutely imperative that there should be no public dissent or any appearance that would suggest disunity with the government. There was a rebellion, but there could be no revolt, and no resignations. I had to keep it quiet.

Events moved quickly. I let it be known that I intended if necessary to kick up a stink, and that I would go as high as I could. I arranged with Denis Allan, Deputy Under-Secretary in charge of the Middle East, that I would go to see Ivone Kirkpatrick the new PUS in the Foreign Office and who was a man of great integrity. Denis said he would go with me. Kirkpatrick was calm and polite, and when I had finished he said: "I have to tell you that there is a total division of opinion between us. My view is that if we don't do anything about this, within a week we shall have the Soviets on the ground and in Cairo in a fortnight." I said I disagreed; Kirkpatrick said his was the view of the Secretary of State and the government.

My only route of appeal after this was the Head of the Home Civil Service, Norman Brook. I knew it would be useless to go to him, but I had said I would do everything I could. One man came to me and said he would resign. Remembering what Eddie Playfair had told me, I told the civil servant that he was not in any way to advertise his reason for leaving. He had to do it on other grounds. Someone very junior out in the Middle East put in his resignation. They were the only two. I feel it was one of my more productive moments though it did not right the situation; the influence to change policy was elsewhere.

Suez was a half-witted, half-baked idea, with terrible consequences, the more so given the speed with which everything took place. We impaired our friendship with the Americans, and destroyed our reputation in the Middle East to the point that it has never completely recovered. I, moreover, had been trying to build up our Middle Eastern Service, and throwing a marmalade pie in the Arabs' face did not help. The cross-section of opinion which I represented rejected outright the idea that they were supporting another Munich and appeasing another Hitler. The likes of Kirkpatrick had been involved in Munich, and it undoubtedly affected their judgement. It was particularly unthinkable that a man so steeped in the Service as Eden could do anything so silly. He was trying to do what he thought Winston would have done. It was a demonstration of virility. Winston would never have done it. It risked our whole position in the world and very quickly brought about the murder and the downfall of the King in Iraq. The war was brought to an end by the refusal of Dulles to support Britain and the breakdown of Eden's health.

Thereafter the Foreign Office was very demoralised. All of us in Whitehall were greatly relieved that we were not abroad and having to publicly defend our government's actions at every juncture. There was little in the way of actual institutional reforms prompted by Suez. We tried to mend our fences, as we usually had to, after wind damage by the politicians. Government backbenchers were the bane of the episode. There was no purge of civil servants, largely because no one knew the extent of dissent. The fallout was confined to Eden, who was a nervous wreck at the time, and had a breakdown soon after, and subsequently resigned. As for the Foreign Office, it really had to rethink its Middle East policies.

Before I finally left the Personnel department I moved on to another hobby-horse. Perhaps the main task, which urgently needed doing when I arrived was someone to make our commercial work more professional and credible to the business world. I was faced with enormous complaints from the Confederation of British Industry that they never received any help from the Foreign Office in their foreign trading. Again I saw myself as an intermediary, and co-operated very closely with the Board of Trade to try and train our people before they went off to commercial posts. I did a lot of work with the Board of Trade and business outfits like the Confederation of British Industry, and courses for diplomats were established.

Progress was slow because the prejudices of business against diplomats, diplomatic habits and Embassies were strong. In the Service itself the prejudice against being incorporated into the rather lowly Service which the Commercial Diplomatic Service had been was deep and persistent. Many Ambassadors knew and cared nothing of economics of any kind. However, we began to provide better training and to increase the popularity of commercial work by selecting good people and promoting them: Tom Brimelow, Donald Tebbitt, Denis Wright, among others. Our success in this, curiously, began to lead to another distortion of the Service. Once it was realised that good commercial officers were useful, the demand for their appointment to every post and even as specialists in almost every sort of commodity, showed signs of growing beyond all reason or financial capacity.

Head of Personnel was my first position of executive authority. It was a bit of a culture shock to begin with, because I did not know what was going to happen, in time-honoured Foreign Office fashion. It helped that I had a first-class Private Secretary, Allison Paul. She had no liking for me at all, and not the faintest idea about people, but had an enormous understanding for what I would like and needed. She would say what meeting was important and what was not. She was very good for me, and put me through the wringer when I started.

The Foreign Office is a funny old outfit. It does not regard a post that is mainly administrative, like mine was, as being worthwhile or serious. They assume one wants to be dashing about wearing cocked-hats. I enjoyed the job, thought it totally worthwhile and absolutely loved every minute. Much of my excitement derived from the realisation that we were building a new Service, with new rules and humanising the Foreign Office. If there had been any form of proper training, my time at Personnel might have been more firmly based and had more practical significance. I felt that people in the Service have to be nurtured, and when I was given the chance I did what I could; to do what I thought Ernie Bevin the co-author of the bible of the new Service would wish. The only time Anthony Eden spoke to me when I ran Personnel was when he told me not to send John Julius Cooper (Norwich) to Moscow, because his mother, Lady Diana Cooper, did not want him to go. I sent him to Beirut instead, where his career changed course and eventually, as a distinguished historian, was very valuable. He might have done much better in Moscow though, for which he had been trained.

TWELVE

Jordan, 1960 to 1962

After eight years, the time had come for me to leave Personnel. I told Derick Hoyer-Millar that I felt I had to go back into a normal job in the Foreign Office. For years I had been deciding people's lives, a dangerously God-like operation. I needed to leave that behind and take my own chances.

I was asked whether there were any posts I would like to go to. The British mission to the United Nations in New York was mentioned again, but I declined. There was a rejection implicit in my decision, though I never thought about it at the time. The number two position in New York was generally regarded as where a diplomat goes who is intended for the top. It was part of the orthodox route of preferment. It suited me much more to go back into a smaller post where I could have close relations with the government, a scenario where I am much more effective. I asked for a place which was not too glamorous, entailing a tinge of hardship. I got my wish and accepted the Ambassadorship in Amman. I was rather young for such a post, but the Personnel department was looking to reward me after what had been a pretty successful period there, and Jordan had been thought to be sufficiently important under my predecessor Charles Johnston, and I certainly regarded it as a plum. I have always thought of myself as an operator in places which were not 100 per cent comfortable: Ethiopia or Egypt were other posts I hankered after.

Amman was both nice and exciting. Jordan was, and remains, a very Anglophile country, though there were people who very much disliked the

Amman, 1960.

British. There was a great deal of sniping at me, through my living high up on a hill next door to the King, and, implicitly, living in the King's pocket. At the time the British Embassy was one of the prestige buildings in Amman, though I had long made it my resolution that if the King wanted it back, we would hand it back. He did eventually want it for his brother Hassan, after I had gone.

Britain had been Jordan's mandate power, and was still at that time our closest ally in the region, though we were beginning to resume our relationship with Egypt after the Suez debacle. Egypt lay alongside and was naturally more important in our eyes. It was also in a strong position to threaten Jordan and it was feared at one time that it might try to gobble Jordan up. Egypt's young officers were ambitious and intrigued with Jordan's younger officers and stimulated Jordan's desire for independence, largely because they were frustrated by Glubb Pasha's apparent control of the King. This had become a real danger for Jordan and the King decided to dispense with Glubb's services and take over command of the army himself. There was great fear that this would move Nasser to take over the Jordan army and Sir Charles Johnstone persuaded the British government that, to avoid this, Britain must give the King the help he needed to assert his independence. This led to support being sent to King Hussein to help him maintain his position and in fact, the take-over of the army by a Jordanian, Habes Majali, originally trained by Glubb, took place quietly and was successful. Jordan unlike most of its neighbours never had any oil and always suspected that it was a horrible plot by the Western powers to deny parity with its neighbours. This was not true at all; there was no oil. Partly because of this I was always having to try to prevent the Jordanians from doing silly things with their money. We had a very strict policy on this. The Jordanians were always asking the Americans to help provide them with a television service or something else which in my view was totally unnecessary. The Americans supported our view for a long time, but then they were persuaded by smart salesmanship that Jordan would benefit and went ahead in providing the help to set up the service.

Our main area of rivalry with the Americans was over arms. We were arming the Jordanian army and had done for some time. It was widely known and was all perfectly legitimate. There were complaints about the arms supplied. My official explanation was that the roads were bad and the

left:
Osla launching
"The England",
Copenhagen, 1963.

below:
Myself, Bahjat
Talhoumi (the Prime
Minister) and King
Hussein at lunch,
November 1962.

shipments were damaged *en route*, but I was always in some doubt about this. We were also arming the Israelis as were the Americans who saw no particular harm in our rivalry in this field. They put up with it in the interests of peace.

I had a military mission with me, as well as inheriting two men who had been with me in Serbia and were from my regiment. Both were very senior to me: Vivian Street, who had been with me in Yugoslavia, and would have become Chief of the General Staff had he lived, and Paddy Bodan. Vivian had been number two to Fitzroy and was a first class soldier. He and Paddy were both extraordinarily good in coping with me as their boss, though they were both senior to me in the army.

My orders were – as quickly as I could and without causing worry to the King – to get rid of both our military and air attachés and impress on the King that he must manage alone instead of being rescued by British troops in a crisis. I soon gave up the idea of getting rid of Bennet the air attaché because the King was so dependent on his help, both in teaching him to fly, and also in training and making plans for the embryo Jordanian air force. But the military mission was less sensitive to the King's personal wishes and plans for its reasonably early withdrawal went steadily ahead with the loyal support of its commander, Brigadier Street. His predecessor had been prone to quietly encourage the King's wish to retain and in fact plan a larger role for it, despite the wishes of London.

Os and I settled in a lovely Embassy house near the Basman Palace looking out over the panorama of the Jordanian capital.

It was not long before a new crisis struck. The most germane fact about Jordan was that its head of state was a King who was only 26 but who had nevertheless been on the throne for nearly a generation. I liked him very much, and we always got on well, and, indeed, continued to keep in touch after I had left Amman. Even by 1961, however, his position was still not entirely secure. He lacked popularity with his subjects, and there was little confidence in him in Washington. Through his education at Harrow and his training at Sandhurst, it was inevitable, however, that we would have some affinity with the King. This affinity became more tangible with a development during my time as Ambassador, but a development which carried considerable risks.

The King suddenly declared that he wished to marry a young British girl,

Toni Gardner whose father was on the military mission. We had heard rumours of a relationship between Toni and the King for some time. They had met at the Amman Go-Kart Club, and before long their engagement was announced. Hussein had already been married, in 1955, to Dina, an Iraqi relation. They had a child, Alia, who had been a friend of my daughter Janey. The marriage had not been a success, and they had divorced before I arrived.

The implications of the King's marriage to a Christian and a Westerner were serious, with virulent Arab nationalists bordering Jordan denouncing British imperialism, and we hastily made enquiries. This was quite a test for me, because marrying an English girl was a dangerous thing for the King of Jordan to do. There was already trouble in the United Arab Republic, where some of the younger Jordanian officers were in cahoots with the Syrians who had a Nasserite commanding in Damascus.

I went to see the King. I advised him that I did not think his marriage would be a very good idea. "It is not for me to interfere, and I am sure that your majesty has thought of everything, but I do wonder whether this marriage is the best thing to do. The only concern of the British government is that your majesty's reign is a success and that you and your people are contented." He very politely pointed out that he knew the woman he wanted to marry, and that, moreover, he had been on the throne for 17 years, while I had only just arrived. I said "I am sure your majesty is right, and I had merely wanted to ensure that you had considered all the possible repercussions. I felt it my duty to mention this". He assured me that he had thought the matter through quite thoroughly, thank you.

Back at the Embassy I had to confront a large faction of the old Arabists and the military attaché, Charles Chaplin. A slight insurrection was launched to the effect that the marriage could not be allowed to take place and wouldn't have happened in the days of Glubb Pasha, who had resigned not long before. I said I could do nothing about it: the King was the King and there it was. A whispering campaign was conducted, which met with my reiteration that I could do nothing about it.

Then I went off to see the Prime Minister, Bahjat Talhouni. I rather liked Bahjat, though he was somewhat corrupt. He met me in his office, in the presence of the Jordanian Commander-in-Chief, a decent straightforward man. They both looked very depressed and sat stroking their beards. The Prime Minister said to me: "We can't stand for this. We can't stand for the King's marriage to a Westerner. You must do something about it Ambassador." I told them I would think about it. "I've already told the King not to marry the girl, and to fully consider all the implications." I promised I would go away and think and see whether I could do anything worthwhile.

I thought that there would be no harm done if I went back to see the King, though I might be asked to leave the country. I could see that the King's action was in fact caused by his need to show who was in charge in Jordan, and I did, after all, rather agree with the Prime Minister, that it was best that he did not marry an English girl. So I went back to see the King, taking a few pills and a deep breath. I said, "Your majesty, I speak with the utmost reluctance, and feel it is a really awful of me to raise this matter again, but I feel I must, as your intended wife is a British subject. I have been under a certain amount of pressure about it", though I mentioned no names; it would not have helped to tell him that his Prime Minister and his Commander-in-Chief had put me up to it. "Our one aim," I continued, "is to ensure your majesty's happiness on the throne, and that there is no trouble of any kind. We all know the type of man Nasser is." The King looked up, and said "Well, I've listened to what you've said, and if you had said it in any other way I'd have asked you to leave. But I won't. I take what you have said in good part. You have been expressing your opinion, and I have to tell you that I am going to disregard it. I've told you already that I need this girl. She's the only one who can make me happy. We shall be married. It is difficult for me and awfully difficult for her, but I feel we must go ahead." I said that I fully accepted his majesty's view, if that was what it was, and thanked him for being so forbearing and kind and withdrew.

The King and Toni were married, and she became Princess Muna al Hussein and converted to Islam. She was quite short, as was the King, so that they made very good partners on the dance floor. The marriage was a success, and though they divorced nine years later, Toni and the King remained friends. Hussein married twice more thereafter, and when he died in 1999 their son Abdullah succeeded to the throne.

After my contortions over Toni Gardiner, there remained a coolness in my relations with King Hussein, though, since I had not been sent back to London, I had not completely blotted my copybook. I told the Foreign

Office what I had done, but they seemed very indifferent. The Foreign Office never takes initiatives of the kind I had risked. If one is an Ambassador and something needs to be done one has to do it on one's own. A few months later, nothing subsequently having happened, the King suddenly decided to have a new government, and sent for Wasfi Tell to be his Prime Minister. Of the two men who had propositioned me, the Prime Minister had gone, and the Commander-in-Chief remained. The King had put together a high class government which was relatively non-corrupt. They were a good lot, and they were friends of mine. I was suddenly on a good wicket.

There was one mildly historic event before my time was at an end, involving Kim Philby. I did not know Philby, though I knew all about him. I knew that he had been involved with the manoeuvres to get Burgess and Maclean out of Britain, and I knew from Personnel that he was still in MI6, but very much on probation. He avoided any moves against him, and nothing had been done to curtail his freedom: he was operating as a stringer for *The Observer*. He had been on ice since Burgess and Maclean were uncovered, and had been implicated by the Labour MP, Marcus Lipton, in 1955. Macmillan stood between him and total exposure, and so he had been granted something of a stay of execution, though Philby had had to leave the Foreign Office in 1951. He had been sent to Beirut for his paper. I got a letter from Nick Elliot, who worked with MI5, commending him as an old friend of his and someone to whom I ought to be kind. He was coming to Jordan with his wife Eleanor. Os and I immediately asked them to lunch at the Embassy.

They duly arrived one day. I have never disliked anybody so much at first sight. He was rotten: drunk, stale, almost mouldy. He had clearly been drinking for a long time; perhaps since the Maclean inquiry. His wife was quite sleazy too. We talked and I found that I knew her vaguely. Since she had been in Germany and Beirut I asked if she knew an old friend of mine, Sam Brewer, from the *New York Times*. She did. They had been married. That shut me up for the time being. Philby went back to Beirut and disappeared later that day, to be rediscovered in Moscow. The episode in every particular left me with an unpleasant taste in my mouth.

It was a lovely summer and we had a number of visits to the Embassy, which we continued to enjoy. Our staff were first rate though constantly pruned by the Foreign Office. I could not have had a better number two and Councillor than Willie Morris and his delightful wife, who as an American was useful in dealing with our American colleagues. The most important was Bill McComber, the Ambassador, who was able, cooperative and helpful. We worked together closely and pressed the interests of our respective countries as hard as we could without too much competition unless they became very important to either of us and had therefore to be tempered. We made, I think, an effective team that worked well together and we encouraged the Jordanians to give thought to other considerations in the future. In a seminar in which the Indians and other important Third World countries played a prominent part, Wasfi Tell initiated an important plan for the re-forestation of the most suitable areas of Jordan, but sadly at this moment I fell ill.

By this time I had been in Amman for two years, rather a short time perhaps, but my health was not terribly good. I drove back through Syria to Beirut with the military attaché, Raoul Lempiere Robin. His mission had come to an end and left, I believe, a strong team to face the future under Willie Morris who had been considerably disturbed to find I had been succeeded by Roderick Parkes whom he had not much liked in Cairo and who had, I thought, been safely found a post somewhere else. Parkes later turned our beautiful garden into a chicken run, from which he sold eggs to the staff. Willie was later to be very properly promoted to Ambassador in Cairo, where 20 years on my second wife and I spent a very happy holiday with Julian and Margaret Bullard on the Nile.

I went to Beirut hospital and was told I had to have my thyroid out. I went back to London through Jordan and Syria with Raoul Robin, where I had the operation. I had said my goodbyes in Amman and did not return. It was rather sad when things were going so well, but difficulties later about the Yemen, and then the disastrous assassination of Wasfi Tell in Cairo after being so briefly Prime Minister and under whom so much progress had been made, made me rather glad to have escaped.

I had enjoyed Jordan, and had felt that things were really getting going and that I was doing quite well. Being removed deflated me.

THIRTEEN

Denmark, 1962 to 1966

I came back to London, and went to see the Foreign Secretary, Alec Douglas Home. He suggested that I should go to Denmark, where I could facilitate their entrance into the Common Market. The post would provide me with a chance to continue the work I had done at Mutual Aid, in the sense of expanding and developing British commercial interests, something I had always wanted to play a part in.

Denmark was not a bad place to go, their doctors were very good, for one thing, and the Danes treat one extremely nicely. Our reception in Copenhagen was certainly auspicious. Most of the domestic press reports noted approvingly that I had already worked out the correct priorities: first I met the King, then I met the press, and finally I met the government. One becomes almost immediately an honorary member of the Danish Diplomatic Service. Copenhagen was not, however, a tremendously prestigious posting. Denmark has of late become rather more prestigious with the growing independence of the Baltic states. At that time, though decent, it was a soft post.

The challenge in Denmark was in negotiating change: the transformation of Europe and the Common Market, and ensuring that there be no major misunderstandings between Copenhagen and London. The Danes were very keen on going in with us; and indeed were very keen on going everywhere with us, not least because we were the main market for their bacon. I made a great speech about our going in to the Common Market together, and it was very well received. Then, two days later, Charles de Gaulle emphatically said "Non". My special mission had failed as soon as I had opened my mouth.

There were still many things to do, and I met, among others, Harold Wilson and Nikita Kruschev. In the main I was associated with trade, though there was also the social aspect. I ran a British Week, which managed to combine the two. Princess Margaret came, as did Tony Snowdon, staying with the Danish royal family, to which they were related. The couple made speeches all over Denmark, and toured factories. I said to Margaret before we started one visit: "Well I expect you will want a brief". She replied, "No, John, I do not want a brief. I am an ace at this sort of thing". She was. They both did very well; it was one time when one could say the British royal family were totally on the right wavelength. I was full of admiration.

Os's sister had known Tony before he married Margaret, and she had said that he was the worst possible person to become a royal: very nice but totally undisciplined. He is a Bohemian, not really tame, and was interested in everything, but always invariably late for everything. But I cannot think of a royal couple better suited to meeting members of the public. Later, as a thank you, Margaret and Tony had us to stay at Windsor, which was great fun, and we went to Ascot in the royal procession. Over the years after her divorce, Margaret deteriorated considerably, and seldom concealed her boredom, as when she visited us at Thornham in 1983.

In Copenhagen they asked to meet the 60 leading Danish men of culture, and it was my job to find them. At home in Britain if one had been charged with such a task there would have been a tremendous row as to who was the best and who was not the best, but there was no problem in Denmark. I called in a professor, and I asked him if he could name 60 and he did.

The British Week involved a great deal of work. My entire staff was involved. London sent us a man to run it, and the Treasury appropriated some funds, which were nowhere near adequate. The central concern was trade, which was why the Export council for Europe was involved, and the likes of McFadyean, Abel Smith, and Sandy Glenn. It was a tremendous advantage that I knew and had good relations with these people, and that I had other links through my efforts at inculcating a commercial awareness in the Service while at the Foreign Office, and, to a lesser extent, when I worked on Mutual Aid.

Though trade was the primary concern in our relations with Denmark, we had done very little about it. Previous British Weeks had garnered great publicity, only to leave a very nasty taste in the Danish mouth as they were left to pick up the bills and the pieces. Several Danes told me that their Mayors had been sacked because they tried to carry out their belief that the British would behave fairly. After the Week was over I had a word with McFadyean and Abel Smith, to try and smooth things over. Trade, of course, went beyond bacon. One highlight of the week was when I compèred a fashion show of top London designers, with the assistance of a lady from *Vogue*. A catwalk was erected inside the Embassy, and the show was followed by an enormous party. We had some football teams out, including Arsenal, but the Treasury was exceedingly reluctant to find the money for such ventures. I had to pay out of my own pocket, and hoped to get it back one day. I did, through the Export Council for Europe.

There was one problem which arose, connected with trade matters. We had reneged on an undertaking given during the negotiations to enter the Common Market, not to impose duty on Danish imports. We tried to tell the Danes that they had got it wrong, and that no such undertaking had been assumed, but they then proceeded to produce the relevant papers to show we were backtracking on something we had promised. There was quite a row, but throughout they behaved extremely nicely, and never took me to task about it at all. They could have been very nasty had they so wanted. As much went for the Cod War. This conflict saw me go out to sea in a Naval Patrol Boat. Contrary to some fears voiced at the time, the crew behaved quite perfectly.

Policy in the main did not noticeably change when a new government was installed in Whitehall.

When the Labour government was re-elected in 1966, George Brown became Secretary of State for Foreign Affairs. George was always doing things behind my back, communicating with the Danes, and muttering "stuff the Ambassador". The reason had as much to do with internal politics at Westminster as in anything to do with diplomacy. The Danish Foreign Minister, Per Haekkerup, used to ask me if I knew what George Brown was up to, and I would reply that I did not and would be grateful if he would enlighten me. He usually did.

In neither of my Ambassadorial posts was there much to write home about. I was useful. In Denmark I played a considerable part in re-establishing a relationship, which had been allowed to go downhill. In Jordan I helped to modernise a post, which had hitherto been run by the soldiers. Most responsibilities were routine, though it is certainly the case that I find a lot of things harder than I should. I find making speeches hard, for instance, though as an Ambassador I was good at them. I had to be.

Of my two Ambassadorships, Jordan could be characterised as one preoccupied with politics, and Denmark with trade. The more exciting one was obvious, as perhaps was the one where I could have greater influence. I was happier in Amman. Denmark was straightforward and though I was always busy no posting could have been happier. Jordan was more interesting, and dicier. There was always the danger of the balloon going up somewhere. In Denmark the balloon would never go up. If I was not underemployed in Denmark, I was probably underwhelmed. Copenhagen was almost exclusively concerned with the Common Market.

On my return to London in 1966, I trod water. I was tired and Osla needed a break. Newly promoted to the rank of Assistant Under-Secretary of State, I took over the Africa department, as usual I had no real knowledge of Africa, with the exception of its north-eastern corner. I was in the post for two years, but remember little about it.

Everyone in the department had reached the pessimistic conclusion that there were three problems that we could never solve: Rhodesia, South Africa, and the Palestinian/Egyptian/Israeli problem. Through having met so many South Africans, I always felt that it was not beyond hope that people might eventually want and be able to work together in South Africa. The department was quite sure, however, that the weight of history was too heavy and reconciliation could not be achieved before everything collapsed in bloody war.

It was for this reason that I was enraged when an echo of the ludicrous Bevin salon was raised. One rule I had learnt was: don't get involved in Arab politics; it never does anybody any good. In 1967 or 1968 I walked into a meeting in the Foreign Office, which was concerned with intriguing to put in one of the Mahdi's family as Prime Minister of the Sudan, which I thought was the kiss of death. We had a spy in the Sudan who thought this was a marvellous idea, and it appealed to various people in the Foreign Office. Ministers were very keen, particularly the Secretary of State for Commonwealth Relations, George Thomson. I could not believe such a straight man would support such a barmy idea. As in 1946 I found myself in a society where I was totally out of place. I thought I should speak up because it was such a wrong thing to advocate, but since they were halfway through the intrigue I kept my mouth shut. Luckily the whole thing died a death.

I had come back from Copenhagen because the Foreign Office thought I was ill. My sickness in Jordan had passed, but not my reputation for illness. My original plan of returning to Personnel came to nothing. Nobody thought of me. It was difficult to nudge people when I was on the continent. The Permanent Secretary, Paul Gore-Booth, whom I liked, was a rather serious Christian Scientist, and was usually unbiddable. He did not help me. I think he felt that my time at Personnel had been too personal. He did not have the confidence in me that I had even in myself; which is rare.

People said to me, "You know, old boy, you must give yourself a chance of getting to the top". For a while I really believed them, and thought I had better do it. I took my chance, and was offered a good post, which, at the age of around 40 was a considerable achievement.

I was offered promotion as Ambassador to Brazil. Such a post was one we dreaded most. On our way to Buenos Aires in 1950 we had stopped at Rio and called in to see the Ambassador, Neville Butler. He had been pleased with his Embassy and showed us round. It was a large house and was still the Embassy until a new site was acquired in Brazilia which was to be the new capital. It struck us that the existing Embassy, which was rather lavish, and needed a fairly large staff, was in a rather inappropriate position: on a hill with rather grand houses around it, on the edge of one of the poorest parts of the city. In 1966 the house had been taken over by the new Labour government to show that it would continue to cope with the sort of formal life Butler described. He said that the Brazilians expected a fairly lavish social life from the Embassy and that a lot of servants were needed. I don't know how many he mentioned, but the figure of 100 seems to stick in my mind. It seemed, from what Butler said, an even more lavish lifestyle than would be expected in Brazilia.

left:
*HM Ambassador,
Copenhagen, 1962*

below:
*At the Embassy,
Copenhagen, 1962*

When we left, after our brief visit in 1950, Os and I had said to ourselves that it was not the sort of post we would ever want to be offered. Its main purpose seemed to be social and we decided then and there that if it was ever offered to us, we would ask to be excused. We felt that, at this stage in our careers, we wanted something a good deal less ostentatious, and with a serious work content. Between our posting in Buenos Aires and the offer of Brazil 15 years later, life had been pretty hectic. When I came home one evening to Os after receiving the telegram suggesting that we should go to Brazil, I went in with my thumbs down. The proposal was a shock.

Curiously enough, given the reason for my withdrawing from Copenhagen and Amman, it was Osla's health, which proved to be a complication. Os had a rather serious illness, and after two consecutive posts abroad could not face another. She said she was far too tired to take on a post like Rio. She said if I could suggest to the Foreign Office that she could have two years off from diplomatic work she would join me later. I felt that I could not go to Rio without her. I would find life impossible alone. I telegraphed the office and said that, while I was grateful for the offer and the promotion it would mean, we could not accept at this stage, and would like another post suggested. Colin Crow, chief clerk at once replied saying that they would if they could find another post for me – or try to find a different sort of job. For the first time in my career, I began to think that it might be wise to seek another sort of job where this sort of conscientious problem did not arise.

Soon afterwards we were back in London and with my knowledge of the Service I suggested that we might be given two years *en disponibilité*. I also asked Paul Gore-Booth, if this could be arranged, and he thought it could. He understood my worries about Osla's health and about my being separated from her at such an important stage in our lives and with a growing family still at home.

A variety of possible other posts were suggested to me in a tentative way. Though it did not necessarily mean a home posting, I required one which was demonstrably better for my wife. I was offered Ireland. At that time Ireland was not very difficult or important. And I did not want to spend my closing years as little more than a host for the Dublin Horse Show. It went to Leonard Figg, who was with me in Amman. Next I was offered Ethiopia, which at another time I would have gladly accepted, just as I would have done Kenya. Willie Morris, a tough, rugged Yorkshireman and my number two in Amman, was Ambassador in Addis Ababa. He wrote from there and I thought it was my cup of tea, but it did not actually materialise.

Meanwhile time passed. Though my request for a sabbatical was agreed in principle by my superiors, a solution became increasingly difficult to find. It was not clear that the Foreign Office had much idea as to what I should do. I had half hoped for Chief Clerk. The Foreign Office felt that they had better give me some preliminary training for Rio and this began to bite into the time that Os and I had expected would be free of diplomatic work. No other suitable possibilities seemed to materialise and I came to the conclusion that I should surrender the idea of Rio in the future and suggested to Os that the best solution might be one that I had always disliked as an option and had recommended that my colleagues should never take unless they were sure that what they hoped to do would suit them, which was to try to find a job outside the Service.

FOURTEEN

The British Council, 1968 to 1972

Os and I started to put out feelers. I heard that I had been shortlisted as Private Secretary to the Queen, a job I would have hated. Os made some casual enquiries, and by chance was told by Lady Albermarle, a Vice-Chairman of the British Council, that I might like to apply for the post of Director-General. Os and Lady Albermarle thought that this might suit us. In Buenos Airies I had known, but not been intimate with the British Council representative Arthur Montague, and I believed they did a very good job, which interested me because it seemed in many ways, to fit with what I had learnt and done with the Foreign Office.

Before taking this any further I told Os that I would want to talk to Lady Albermarle because I had heard that the British Council did not much like the Diplomatic Service, even though they worked alongside them. I therefore told her I was interested, but needed to be quite sure before putting my name forward, that the Council would be ready to accept and work with me. She said she would have to consult her colleagues and, after consulting the Chairman of the Selection Board for the post, Lord Bridges (the Cabinet Secretary) and Paul Sinker, who was quite a friend of mine on the Civil Service Commission, I received the answer that I would be very welcome in the job and would, in fact, be a strong candidate. Paul Sinker indeed went so far as to say that though the Board of the British Council were not necessarily looking for a candidate outside the British Council, he knew things about their internal candidate that he might later reveal to the British Council Selection Board. I soon arrived at the view that it was the best possible place for me, as it would be my last post.

I was attracted, for I felt, and still do, that with Britain's declining status, suspicions of our imperial motives in the Third World, and the increasing conduct of much diplomatic work through multilateral agencies, that the Council, which I had admired abroad, offered possibly the best chance of doing constructive work to promote and enhance British influence abroad. At a time of tension around the world between East and West, this was an organisation concerned with helping others and establishing trust. I felt that my long stint in Personnel had enabled me to know and be trusted by many senior people in the Diplomatic Service and that I could thus help to overcome the mutual suspicions which sometimes bedevilled relations between them and the British Council. The Institution had existed in a strange state of semi autonomy. The appointment of the boss required the approval of both the Foreign Secretary and the Prime Minister. I went on to discuss the matter with the Permanent Under-Secretary and others in the Foreign Office who were amongst my closest friends there. They all expressed real sorrow that I should feel it necessary to take this step and tried to dissuade me, but agreed that if I were determined to go ahead and could not get the sabbatical from Diplomacy that I had asked for, I should put my name forward. I think in fact that the Foreign Office was sad to see me go, but had a problem with overcrowding. Therefore they were not as loath as they pretended to see me go if I could find another job which suited me.

I had felt that my qualifications, character, and experience were very different from Sinker's, as were my ambitions. I wanted to make the Council, which seemed on the outside to have slightly authoritarian tendencies, into a happier and more democratic organisation. Sinker, who had run the Council under his personal command, said that hitherto he had perhaps been regarded as unsympathetic to the more democratic tendencies which had come in after the war. But he thought the time had come for the Council to grow up and learn how to carry this burden. I gathered that the view of the Council was that a bit more dash and panache was required and that my experience seemed likely to provide this.

Curiously enough, when they interviewed me, their questions were remarkably simple and did not seek to explore what, if anything I had to offer. I had expected to be asked and would have been glad to discuss, what I had achieved in running Personnel. I realised that I would have to produce a warmer relationship between the Board of the British Council and its staff. I felt that the value the government seemed to attach to the British Council was too small, and thought that I could, with my diplomatic experience, enhance that value. To this, my recent experience in implementing the report produced at the end of the war by Eden and Bevin, on which I had been working for 10 years – doing the administrative work connected with it, had given the Foreign Office and those with whom I dealt, some confidence in my capacity in this field. I hoped to convince the British Council of the importance the Foreign Office placed on their activities.

I dare say that my views at that time would have put off the Council from selecting me if I had been asked to express them, but I was not asked and there was thus no chance of anyone, including the members of the Board, knowing what sort of experience I had to offer. This included the incorporation into the Foreign Office of the separate Services which had previously existed under its wing. I had also presided over the period during which the India Office was being steadily Indianised and some of its staff had been made available to us for postings outside India. Soon afterwards, as Sudan started to be Egyptianised, its staff also became available for posting and provided, like the Indian Service, a valuable supplement to our training in Middle Eastern languages and administration.

It would have been at least useful to have a statement of what the Council saw as the main attributes I had to offer, but they agreed, without demur, to follow Lord Bridges, who proposed at the beginning of the last selection meeting, that I was by far the best candidate they had seen and should be appointed forthwith. There had, I understood, been some worry on the Board when the Prime Minister, Harold Wilson, had appointed Lord Fulton as Chairman of the British Council. Bridges, who had been a participant in some of the greatest decisions of the war, said that he would settle any differences between the Board, the Foreign Office, and the Prime Minister, before he went into retirement. He accordingly, at his last meeting got the Board to agree to my appointment as Director-General and then immediately went into retirement.

One fact that I did not know and on which I sought reassurance, was whether the British Council would be prepared to accept someone like me who was a devoted member of the Foreign Service. I had been assured by Lady Albermarle, who had consulted Bridges and Sinker who knew me very well in my dealings with the Civil Service Commission, that I would be very acceptable to the Council. They both said that the only possible internal candidate from the Council's staff, Reg Philips, would be thought unacceptable by Sinker.

After I was appointed, I was amazed to find a mass of papers from British Council staff objecting to any idea of someone from outside the Council being brought in as Director-General. Their plea appeared hardly to have been listened to by the Treasury but at that time the Treasury seldom listened to the advice of any department wishing to comment on leadership being proposed to them.

I later discovered that at the last Interview Board before my appointment, Fulton had commented on the decision to appoint me, that he felt the British Council would be very suspicious of again appointing an outsider and not a member of the British Council as Director-General, and that he felt that it might be particularly dangerous to appoint a member of the Diplomatic Service since the British Council was sensitive about being seen to be independent and not merely a part of British foreign policy. He was immediately challenged by Lord Bridges who asked him if he had any other suggestion. Did he or did he not think I was the best candidate they had seen. Fulton immediately withdrew his objection and agreed to the Board's decision. I'm afraid it was at that moment that my fate was sealed, though I took several years to recognise it.

When I found out about the protest from the staff side, I felt a bit betrayed and toyed seriously with the idea of withdrawing my candidature. It seemed a bit rash to do this and I consulted two very good heads of department under me and who were concerned about my future: Denis Spears, who was working on Egypt and Martin Le Quesne, who dealt with Africa and was in every way first class. Denis said that he thought it would be pretty arrogant if I withdrew before being told I was acceptable. I took his advice.

Sinker immediately suggested that I should quickly go off on a tour to see some Council posts overseas and to try to understand what I had taken on. I was given a programme, which included Rio, Buenos Airies, Chile, Uganda, Addis Ababa, Sudan and Egypt, before returning home. I had been advised to leave Osla behind because she had signs of cancer and was not well, though her involvement with the Council would be important.

I was particularly impressed by Rio, with Roddy Cavaliero in charge, with Addis and Sudan especially and Egypt, where Harold Beeley was Ambassador. With a very interesting and friendly Egyptian Minister of Culture, we negotiated the first stages of an invitation to bring the Tutankhamun Exhibition to London in return for a visit to Cairo of the Royal Ballet, instead of a rather small sculpture by Reg Butler which the Council had planned as their contribution to Cairo's forthcoming millennium celebration. When the visits later took place they were a great success and rather mitigated the poor impression our original proposals had made in Cairo.

I returned as quickly as I could to London to set up my Private Office and to take charge. In an entirely new job this naturally took some time. This was followed fairly quickly by a meeting of the senior officers in the Council to welcome me. I'd already been asked by the Press to comment and said how glad I was to have been offered the job. My first formal meeting of the Council staff was glacial. Paul Sinker had told me that he had treated the staff distantly and formally and while allowing them to contribute to policy, had not allowed them any real part in making it. Any different attitude had to be approached gradually.

I realised at the first meeting when the congratulations and welcome were so low key and half hearted, that there was a lot to do. But I also felt at the same time that I would not try to go too fast until I knew them better and really began to understand what was needed. The basic trouble was that there was no one in the Council that I knew as well as my colleagues in the Foreign Office or could trust, with the exception of my loyal Personal Assistant, Barbara Peake, and the Secretary of the Council, Irvine Watson, a very nice but quiet and discreet person, with whom I could ever have a confidential discussion. It was, for someone of my temperament a position of almost unimaginable agony. I did my best and soon work began: discussions of matters that I hardly knew, and discussions where I started from the edge of the pond. The first was a meeting scheduled with the Duncan Committee, an enquiry headed by Sir Val Duncan, which was examining the Council and other British institutions. It was, I thought, a very successful meeting with two old friends of mine: Robert Wade-Gery and Frank Roberts. When we left, I said to the British Council representatives who had accompanied me – Philips, Gummer and Fowells – that I thought it had been a success. They replied at once and gloomily saying that they would never have talked as I had done. This sort of reaction was almost invariably what I received from my senior colleagues to anything I said in public. It was very daunting to anyone like myself who is not full of self confidence. It was with me as a constant cloud.

My next foreign excursion was a visit to Pakistan while Lord Fulton made a more VIP visit to India. Pakistan was a reasonable success and there were several friends of mine in the Embassy, but the domestic politics were very volatile at that moment, with the Prime Minister on the verge of being forced out. Since it was not thought safe for an official diplomat to visit the Prime Minister, I was sent as a safe substitute.

On my return to London I had to go into hospital for an operation. After I returned to work Philips, Gummer and Fowells asked to come and see me and said quite bluntly, that they did not feel that they could work with me. I asked them how they could say that when they hardly knew me. Philips said that he did not need to tell me; it must be obvious. I said that it wasn't. Philips added that Lord Fulton knew of, and I assumed approved of, their visit to me.

A few weeks later Lord Peart, Lord President of the Council, established a Select Committee to enquire into the British Council. I was called in to see Fulton who told me that he would like to give evidence to the Committee and that I should also do so whenever I wished. I had been told by Sinker that the Council's Chairman, Lord Fulton, had an honorific and part time job with the Council, and that I was entirely responsible for policy and administration. Fulton began the meeting friendly enough, and said that, as the Committee would be meeting shortly, he would like me to give him a full report on what the British Council was doing and where it should be going. I stalled, and said I had only just returned from a long tour abroad and a period in hospital, but that with staff help I would try to produce a few ideas, it being far too early for me to produce the sort of report that he requested. He agreed that if I did this it would be considered at the next meeting of the British Council Board. I got a few selected members of staff, including Reg Philips, to start to think of a few ideas. The response was very slow and half-hearted but just about passed muster.

The Select Committee began their deliberations by a long enquiry into the manner of my appointment and whether it had been at the insistence of the Foreign Office. When Fulton was interviewed, his reply that it had been as a result of a "trawl" of suitable candidates, encouraged the Committee to dig deeper than they had intended, but the Chairman fortunately prevented the Committee pursuing this too far. The report of the enquiry, when it came out several months later questioned how I had been selected but did not object to my selection. Philips told me openly that he did not think I could survive. I asked him why not since my appointment had been approved. But from this moment when I went abroad to undertake a long planned tour of the Council's work in West Africa lasting about four months, Fulton's opposition became open and whole-hearted. I tried as a last gasp, to assemble a small committee from the Treasury consisting of two senior officers, Moore and McCosh, to look into the terms under which I was appointed. I have since learnt that this report was put under restricted embargo for 30 years: normal publication date of government papers. An extraordinary move!

At this point I decided to turn to the adviser Paul Gore-Booth had told me would be my main help if I had any trouble in the Council – Lord Goodman. Goodman was at the time regarded as a wizard, easily able to clear up any problems. I told him of the visit of the three controllers who had said they couldn't work with me. I had warned them that if they really couldn't work with me I would have to find them suitable posts abroad. From the start I had handled Philips – whom I knew to be very disappointed at not getting my job – very gently, suggesting various ways of compensating him for the extra work he had had to do in briefing me. It had no apparent effect. I said to Goodman that I did not think I could send these officers abroad without the agreement of the Board. He agreed and said he would consult those most concerned and tell me the result.

Several months elapsed before Goodman returned to say that my idea of sending overseas the four senior officers who could not work with me could not be approved by the Council Board. Goodman strongly advised me not to persist with my suggestion, and to think of any other steps I could take. He added that in his consultation he had found no support for me. He had also asked Fulton, as I had requested, to undertake not to lead a rebellion, as he recently appeared to have done. In telling me this, Goodman said rather ruefully that we had underestimated the importance that Fulton had attached to becoming Chairman of the Council which, added to his recent report on the Civil Service, would give him great influence in promoting any co-operation between government, education and politics in Britain.

Fulton had given an equivocal reply promising that he would not lead a faction against me unless what I proposed to do was likely to cause serious harm to the Council. I half hoped this half-hearted promise would deter Fulton from coming out too strongly against me. In reporting in this way Goodman had effectively revealed to me that my number was up.

The signal from Lord Fulton about his doubt about my suitability was welcomed by many within the Council, and they quickly got down to the task of dislodging me. There was little chance thereafter of winning the battle. I have always felt that I should then have withdrawn from the Council or have found ground on which to stand and fight. But I had from the start decided that I would not take any action that would embarrass either the Foreign Office, who had treated me very well or the British Council who had shown confidence in selecting me. Neither the Council nor the Foreign Office were held in general esteem by the public and news of a row between two departments would have done both of them a lot of harm. Fulton's appointment would not last forever and the Council were unlikely to maintain an unwavering front. I was wrong.

It was from this moment that Fulton's opposition came blatantly into the open. When I left for Africa, a long trip lasting three or four months, I knew my position was precarious and from that moment Fulton discarded his disguise. Immediately I returned from my tour I realised something was afoot in the way I was treated by staff. I had hoped when I left for Africa that though I was in great danger, Fulton would not dare to go as far as urging my immediate departure, because the legacy left by Bridges, when he retired was to see me carefully into my new responsibilities. Bridges' reputation was such that no civil servant could refuse to carry out his instructions. But I no longer had any time in which to fight on.

Fulton asked me and my wife to come and see him. At that meeting he opened by saying that he had consulted the senior controllers in the Council and that all but one had agreed that my early departure should be requested. I then pointed out that I was not a rich man and could not afford to support my family without a pension. He neither expressed regret nor shame at what he had done. I am quite sure that if Fulton had offered me the sort of deal that is now often made to staff who are unwanted I would have accepted it and gone without further ill feeling, but Fulton refused even to mention or to respond to my request.

I realised that my reputation was in rags. Sir Joe Garner, who was alternately Permanent Under-Secretary and Head of the Diplomatic Service, visited me at this point to ask whether I knew that, on a tour Philips and King, the Deputy Director-General of the Council, had made to India, they had used the opportunity to say that I had gone mad and could no longer be relied upon. I told Joe Garner, who had been told by his son, that what he told me was not a surprise.

Os and I decided that in order to prevent the matter becoming public and therefore doing great damage, I should put forward my resignation and offer to leave in April 1972. This would give enough time to select a suitable successor to take my place. When I rang to say that I planned to take this course I heard that Lord Fulton's contract had come to an end and would not be renewed.

Leslie Rowan, who had, to my great good fortune been appointed to succeed Fulton as Chairman, was well known to me when I had been in Ernest Bevin's Private Office and he was working as Private Secretary to Winston Churchill as well as chairman of the committee handling Marshall Aid. He was sympathetic and he told me that he would if I wished support my continuing as Director-General. I said that I could not possibly accept. It was easy to destroy a reputation and I had been denounced by Fulton to my staff both at home and overseas, and they would never be able to support or believe in me in the future. It would be best, at this stage, to make a clean break, leaving enough time for the Council to make a new appointment and to forget the whole matter. I agreed with Osla that I should issue a statement that for personal reasons, which included her health, and could not therefore be enquired into, I had decided to resign.

I had hoped for some redress from the McCosh report but it never came, and the best thing was to make sure that this episode in British Council history was dead and buried never to be repeated. When after my retirement, I asked a few of the more friendly controllers why they had destroyed me, some managed even to say that it might be a relief for me to return to my comfortable Estate in Suffolk. Some have always believed in fairies. My last weeks at the Council were ruined by a constant stream of the senior Council officers through my office apparently to reassure themselves that I had decided to leave, with several of them threatening to warn the press of the breakdown in the Council if I didn't go. The most senior officers still operating in the Council and a friend of mine gave a small farewell party, which was attended by no other controller.

What has worried me particularly is that as far as I can see, there has been no real change in the structure of appointments since I left. This came to my attention forcibly when I happened to hear of Dr. David Drewery's appointment as Director-General some two years ago, and that he had been forced to withdraw after apologising to senior members of the British Council's staff for interfering in the administration of the Council. This seemed to indicate that any attempt to put the Council's affairs into new hands would continue to be vigorously and successfully opposed by the staff as in my case, and would be supported by the Board. I tried through my resignation to ensure that the Council could start afresh with the appointment of a new Director-General to carry out reforms without meeting the combined and vigorous defence of existing practices. If new policies are wanted by the British Council, its old methods of resisting change will have to be altered. It is perhaps the failure to explore new approaches which has caused so much disappointment to those like Jon Snow and his co-signatories, who wrote to *The Times* recently about the failure to fund the Council adequately to fulfil its potential in the world today.

I continue to believe that the British Council's role in our relations with foreign countries is still vital and could easily be developed with co-operation between the departments. There is a great deal to be done in this field, but the Council seems temporarily to have cut itself adrift from developing this work.

I never felt any animosity to people in the Council except for Fulton and Gummer, whom I felt were moved by malice and not the natural fear of change or disappointed hopes. I had little respect for Fulton and found myself always unable to talk to him; in any serious conversation he resorted to sociological jargon, which came straight from the Tavistock Institute where he was much involved. He seemed keener to dodge rather than face up to difficulties. It has been an unhappy experience to write this account of what happened at the British Council. It is over 35 years ago but I have been persuaded to set down clearly what happened and why. I have done this as best I can after a long gap in which I have had another very happy marriage and have turned my attention to other things, because I believe that much of what happened then was not what the British Council was trying to achieve or I was expected to put into effect. I think a lot of people know or have guessed what happened, but I am the only one who really knows; why should my version be believed?

When we came back from Denmark, Os had a thorough medical examination. She had not been at all well for some time. She was not really ill, but I think she had been sickening for cancer. The examination found nothing. Some time later, in Sloane Street, her leg gave way and she was taken by a doctor to his waiting room, and again given a clear bill of health. On the very day that I retired, Osla had an exploratory operation. I had insisted on the operation, to make sure that she had nothing more serious than the hypoglycaemia she had had for years. The doctor begged me not to go ahead with the operation, but I insisted. A cancer that was thought to be benign was found. Treatment brought a year's happy remission before it worsened. By the spring of 1974 she started to be ill again. The doctors told me there was no hope. We agreed they should do their best to make her end as comfortable as possible. After a long but not painful illness having done as much as she could, she quickly faded away. There was not much that could be done in those days. Cancer advanced pretty quickly. She died in October 1974. It was an enormous blow to me. She was not only really beautiful but that adjective covers her character. She is someone I find difficult to think can ever be replaced in this world. Two years after I lost my career, I had lost my main purpose in life.

FIFTEEN

Recuperating, 1972 to 1980

The nearly simultaneous experience of the British Council and Osla's death almost broke me. Yet I still hankered after public service, both for its own sake and to occupy myself in what I feared would be a long and rather empty future. The British Council came as a tremendous shock. I had always been pleased with the reputation I had built in the years in the Personnel department and on being able to get on with almost anyone. The sadness of this cast a shadow which is only now disappearing. I was just plain ashamed of myself. I had no excuse for my sudden disappearance from my normal life. It did much to darken the years of Osla's illness which began very soon after, almost on the day I left the British Council, and for which no one on the staff even expressed the faintest sympathy though I believe she had there, as everywhere else, been loved and would be missed right down to the humblest.

The whole episode cut my life in half, hitherto I had been busy, happy and on my way upwards and feeling that I still had a useful contribution to make to a Service where I had been very happy and felt that even without Osla I had quite a lot to offer. I could not hope for justice or serious understanding of what I had been through. It was at the last moment that I received the news that Fulton's period at the Council was finished and that he was not to be re-appointed. Perhaps I thought that it had been arranged by such supporters as I had in the Foreign Office, particularly Denis Greenhill. But Fulton's disappearance came far too late. By that time my reputation such as it was, was in tatters and no one else would want to consider employing me.

I was offered a job as Director of the charitable foundation set up by the three Wates brothers with money they had earned from providing housing near London and in building the Mulberry Harbour used so successfully on D-Day. It was a great relief to get away from the atmosphere of calumny and hatred which had surrounded me on all sides, and gave me a new impetus to learn about the sort of charities that had been created and which had done so much good in relieving poverty and distress. I believe that I owed my appointment to Lord Goodman who knew Ifor Evans, the Director of the Wates Foundation whom I was to succeed. Ifor was very helpful and kind, as were the Wates family who since the death of the eldest brother Norman, had a board of trustees consisting of Ronald, Alan, and Norman's eldest son Neil. They could not have been more generous in offering their support and encouragement through those dark days.

I entered a completely new scene; getting to know the poorer areas of London and the needs of their communities. All the Wates family were anxious for new ideas and adventure and urged me – and perhaps Neil especially – to get out and find things that really needed help. I loved this. It kept me very active. It gave me an excuse for asking all sorts of questions and to urge all sorts of people to get on with suggesting new lines we could follow. The Wates had been one of the earliest supporters of Dame Cicely Saunders, the founder of the hospice movement. There were lots of other things; a need for help in Northern Ireland for one, and I went over to explore the peace initiatives already taken in different communities. We worked abroad in the Commonwealth and elsewhere – and here my Foreign Office training was useful – to find and develop schemes which might last and help communities to help themselves, such as Schumacher's Intermediate Technology (the technology was often of a very simple kind and enabled a village for example to sink a well or market their products). We helped medical research in King's College Hospital and projects such as All Faiths for One Race in Birmingham which in those days was run by Clare Short. It was a new and exciting life and one which I really relished and which brought me, as I hunted the land for people and ideas, a new host of friends amongst whom we set up a panel of experts who could help the trustees with their grant giving. I loved it and was happy again, and my office in Toynbee Hall in East London was central to many community and race relations projects being run in that area. I left the Wates Foundation in 1977 when Julia and I were married and we moved back to Suffolk.

The Mental Health Review Tribunal, with which I was involved for five years, was not really much good because it was connected with the crimes of those who had committed rather frightening things as a consequence of their mental health. This meant that no Home Secretary was likely to let anybody out of prison to live a normal life. It was therefore difficult to give real advice, and most of what we did depended on the advice of experts. Our Chairman was a lawyer, who did not have much experience in such matters. The most we could do in practice was amend the regime in which people were held.

When I left the Wates Foundation I was immediately asked to be a trustee or a director of a number of grant-giving charities in London, as well as other bodies in the voluntary sector. All conformed with my long-standing interests and were all designed to mitigate various forms of deprivation and interacted at various levels. For 20 years I was the government nominee to the governing body of the City Parochial Foundation, the large charity involved with poverty in London, and voluntary bodies which were close to or dependent on it. City Parochial was involved with a community language centre and ethnic groups in and around Earls Court. The Trust for London was its offspring, and the Tudor Trust was also involved in that area. We helped Somalis, Kurds, Vietnamese and every sort of refugee community in London, particularly those who knew nothing of British ways and had no other friends.

I was Deputy Chairman of Toynbee Hall under Jack Profumo and I was also asked to run, for the Department of Health, a very good community scheme; Intermediate Treatment. I succeeded Lord Hunt as Chairman in 1985 and resigned in 1990, when at the age of 75 I thought it time to retire from a body dealing with juveniles. I had been on the Parole Board and knew a little about penal policy. I felt when I was asked that I should try to help, and with a small staff we had a lot of success at little cost, diverting juveniles from crime by giving them other things to do and getting them to understand the harm their crimes had done. When I became Chairman a lot of the pioneering had been done, seeds had been sown, the ground cultivated, good practices had already been established though within wide limits there were great variations. In 1988 we celebrated the Fund's tenth anniversary. Our aim was to cover as much of the country as possible, trying to start projects or improve them where the Intermediate Fund was still in its infancy, elsewhere to reassure and encourage projects which were well underway, and to call attention to their successes and strengthen cooperation between local agencies. With committee members Julia and I travelled through most of England. Everywhere the response was really exhilarating. We went to the North-East, and there were excellent projects in very difficult circumstances in Sunderland, South Shields and Durham; in Cumberland there were promising beginnings in an area where Intermediate Treatment had hardly started. Devon and Cornwall had gone further and were very active, while Liverpool had a wide variety of good projects including a fine city farm and a go-cart club. In Cambridgeshire and Essex, there were a lot of very good schemes with the magistrates particularly well informed, supportive, and satisfied. In Basildon, working with the Catholic church, Intermediate Treatment had reduced in one year, the number of girls taken into care from 20 to none. Birmingham and London, particularly in Hounslow, demonstrated very sophisticated schemes and in the latter, an interesting natural overlap between juveniles and young people in the next age group above them.

Such visits were I think valuable in ways which were similar to those I had often undertaken when an Ambassador. The visit of an outside authority alerted the press and local authorities and made them aware, and even proud, of activities which were going unnoticed in the community, but were seen suddenly to be of interest to the outside world. The Fund's association too, with the John Hunt Award Scheme, had much the same affect of bringing to light and public attention and giving some support to initiatives which had been entirely developed locally. Some were splendidly imaginative.

When establishing the Fund, the government wisely decided that it should "match" its government subsidy by getting grants from charities and other private sources. The Fund had done this with great success. In my time it received no more than £500,000 from government in any year; if it wanted any more the only solution was to turn to private charity. It was, I believe, very cost effective. The money saved by keeping offenders out of prison certainly exceeded the subsidy many times over.

So it was to me a great shock and cause of despair when Virginia Bottomley who was Minister of Health in Mrs. Thatcher's government suddenly removed our funding as an economy measure. Lord Elton, who was about to succeed me as Chairman of the IT Fund, started a new Charity called Divert which took on the work of the Fund in preventing youth offending, and is currently joining with the Rainer Foundation (now RPS Rainer) of which I was also a Vice-Chairman and which also works with local communities and helps with young people leaving care.

In all these capacities I have, I hope, done something to respond to the government's call for the "active citizen" to play a part in the solution of social problems. I have certainly seen a lot of them and have reached the very firm conclusion that it is only when all agencies, both public and private, involved in any area of social service, co-operate, that real progress can be made. I have worked closely with all agencies concerned in the penal system – police, probation, prison service, social services, local government, and magistrates – as well as in the community – the Church, sporting bodies, doctors, youth services, teachers, lawyers, businessmen and a wide network of voluntary helpers.

While I was running Wates, Neil did what Ralph Stevenson had done 30 years before; Neil Wates's sister had been at school with Julia Poland, and they remained friends. Neil had also kept in touch with her, and asked me if I could find her a job. Her marriage had collapsed and she had three children to support. I had known a Poland in the Civil Service, and did not like him at all, so I did not follow the matter up very enthusiastically. Two years later Neil came to me and asked how I had been getting on with Julia. I said I was not doing very much, but that my secretary was about to leave for a job in the social services. With Os dying I was, to put it mildly, distracted, and I needed someone as a PA, and, since Neil kept raising the subject, I gave Julia a ring, and we arranged to meet.

Julia arrived one Monday morning, fairly trembling with fear. We got on very well. I needed someone to answer the phone and such like, and she had a very nice voice. She said it was no good: she could not do short-hand, lived in Ashford in Kent, a two hour train journey away, and didn't think she could cope with commuting and looking after her three teenage daughters. I took out a train timetable, and arranged for her hours to coincide with the train times and her family responsibilities. She would catch the 8.15 and come to work at 10.00, and leave at 4.00. She started the following Monday. She later said a guardian angel had guided her to that meeting.

It was a very difficult time for me, as I was completely preoccupied with Os, and I rarely went in to the office, which Julia kept running. Os died around a month after Julia started work; they never met. Our professional relationship blossomed and we began to see each other socially.

About two years after Julia had started working for me, I took her to a performance of *Der Rosenkavalier*. It was her first visit to the Royal Opera House, Covent Garden for many years. It was magical. That evening I introduced her to various friends of mine. Then, after the performance, I proposed to her. I romantically chose the car park of Ashford railway station.

During the first years of our marriage, I took Julia around the world on holidays to all my postings, and met many of my old friends. It was important to me that Julia knew something of my life, and was introduced to the people who matter to me. She says she regrets not having been a part of it, but I suspect Julia would not have appreciated the peripatetic lifestyle, and the constant activity. She is quite a domestic person, and that side to her would be central to the next stage in our life, while Os had reached the stage of her life where, even if she had lived, she would not have been willing or able to take over Thornham the way Julia did. I know Julia loved Thornham and she said that coming here for the first time was, apart from coming home, like going back in time 100 years. She is by nature a builder, and so much of the work of restoring Thornham was quite natural to her; rather than it being an enormous undertaking, she saw one thing as leading logically on to another, though so much of what we did was experimental. It was fortunate or rather imperative, that we shared a love of conservation, gardening, and the natural world.

It was the first time in my adult life that I had not been part of a large machine, in which I could delegate whatever I wanted to delegate; now I was the machine, and was totally responsible. It became a second distinct career for me though I did not realise that when I began.

SIXTEEN

The final chapter

I took over the Thornham Estate from my father in 1980 when he died aged 97. I had inherited it from my Uncle Charles when he died, but my father ran it while I worked abroad and in London. The development of the Estate followed on seamlessly from my years of charity work and was my response to the problems of the area. Julia and I had both been brought up in the now old-fashioned but fundamental Christian belief that the fortunate should share with their less fortunate neighbours. As owner through no virtue of my own, of a lovely Estate, we felt especially blessed. We had worked in the deprived urban areas, and seen the rigours of life there and saw in Thornham a unique opportunity to help people in real need. We thought we could and should build on our experience and the location and capacity of the Estate to develop a resource, responding in as many different ways as possible to the needs of the local and wider community.

In the 1980s unemployment was a major national concern, and locally jobs, mainly in agriculture, were in decline. At the start of the century, when Thornham began to fail as an economic concern, there were about 10 important country houses within 10 miles, all of which have since disappeared, and all of which provided jobs and a way of life. We sought to provide jobs and resources, to invigorate the local communities and involve them in their countryside and gradually to diversify some of the Estate's traditional activities. In this we were encouraged by the Structure Plan for Suffolk, which called attention to the complete absence of amenities around Eye. We seemed in an ideal position to respond. There was, despite isolated examples elsewhere, a good deal that was experimental.

When my grandfather inherited at the end of the nineteenth century, the Estate had been some 40,000 acres. By the 1970s it had been reduced to 2000 acres with substantial land sales after the First and Second World Wars. During the Second World War, the Estate was used for the war effort. There was a radio post in the woods and Thornham Hall served as divisional headquarters. Italian prisoners of war were housed in huts in the old garden and woods. There are now around 1,200 acres of arable land, 400 acres of woodland, ponds and parkland and a river, the Dove flows through it. The Estate contains two small villages; Thornham Parva and Thornham Magna and is bordered by five others; Gislingham, Mellis, Yaxley, Wickham Skeith and Stoke Ash.

Julia and I had married in 1976 and came to live at Red House where I had lived as a boy. The house, which started as two clay lump cottages in the sixteenth century, had traditionally always been lived in by the Agent, and is set in the middle of the Estate yard, with the model nineteenth-century farm buildings around it. When I was a boy, the yard was the base for the Estate workers, where they ate their lunch and reported to the Estate office – the carpenters, the farrier, the sawmill men, the horsemen, the cowmen and the keepers. The engine that drove the mill chugged away in the south-east corner.

In 1976 the yards had largely fallen into disuse and disrepair. The Red Poll herd had all but disappeared, but there were still 13 men working on the farm, in the woods and on maintenance. There were two keepers and the farmyard was a busy place. The Estate and its unspoilt beauty made it a unique oasis of woodlands and fields that were unlike the open prairies of a lot of East Anglia. We were very conscious that local people had nowhere to walk and that their children had nowhere to explore and experience the natural world around them. Farming subsidies took away hedgerows, field margins, cart-ways and rough corners. We felt very strongly that we should share what we were so very fortunate to have, and that by sharing, people would begin to understand and value the natural world and help to preserve it. This was at the beginning of growing awareness by the public of the importance of conservation for the environment. We recognised how vulnerable Thornham was to the forces of change and economic necessity.

All the elms died in our first two years. Great trees that bordered nearly

The wedding, 9th May 1976.

Victoria Poland, Charles H.-M, Bruce Williams, Laurence Trender, J. H.-M., J. H-M., Dick H.-M., George Mason, Mark H.-M. Kate Poland

Caroline Poland, Elizabeth Mason, Janey H.-M., Nancy H.-M.

Alison Williams (Maguire), Mat Williams, Ed Williams, Lesley H.-M., Ann Trender

The entrance to the Walks, Thornham, 1985.

Julia, with a basket of Lady Henniker apples, 1991. (Daily Telegraph).

Receiving degree of Hon. Doctor of Civil Law, University of East Anglia, 1989.

all the field hedgerows and lined the cart-ways. It was a devastating change to the scale of things, reducing the skyline in some cases to the height of elder bushes and hawthorn trees. We were advised to demolish the old farm buildings; modern farming needed larger barns and silos. The village had an ageing and declining population as the younger generation left to find work and better housing in the town. None of the cottages had indoor sanitation and with rents at nine shillings and sixpence per week (50 pence) there was no way we could fund their modernisation.

We took advice about converting the yards into craft workshops; which seemed to be the need in those days, and for cottages for pensioners and some newcomers. We sold the village houses to their tenants, hoping against hope that we could retain the people in the village community and that they would not be tempted to sell on to weekenders. We built, in partnership with Suffolk Rural Housing, a group of sheltered cottages in the Street, and inserted five larger family houses for newcomers, who would, we hoped provide a mix of ages and incomes. We were also very concerned to keep two sites as business workshops so that there was some community life going on and the Street didn't become a museum piece. Twenty years on the balance still holds, but for how long we can't tell.

Meanwhile along with the frantic replanting, which still continues, of hedges, clumps and copses and rows of hardwood, in order to replace the elms and improve the condition of the nooks and corners that were not part of the forestry operation, we began to convert the yards. The local authority, after initial suspicion of our motives, were immensely helpful, even though this was years before the conversion of farm buildings to business premises was even thought of, let alone funded by grant aid. But as we entered the first recession in the 1980s the very small businesses that had established themselves here found it very difficult to survive without the help of "rent holidays".

We had opened the Walks and with a sudden burst of enthusiasm for the environment we had a lot of visitors coming and no-one to tell them where they were going, or to cut out the paths which became impassable in the summer. So we approached the Countryside Commission, who had urged us on to create the public access (with no capital grants to build the lavatories, car parks and other necessities obviously needed by visitors) and they did, in partnership with the Local Authority, fund the salary of a Warden.

This was an enormous relief to us, as order was established, maps printed, waymarking signs put up and we were protected from the frontline and given some privacy. There was no way to collect any entrance money to pay for all this, so we had to rely on people's generosity and voluntary contributions, which never amounted to much, even though there was an unwelcome element among our visitors who assumed we were coining money.

We also came to realise that many of our visitors had little idea of what they were enjoying and wanted to know more about trees, birds, animals and flowers and sometimes about the farm and the history of the Estate. Children, who now were driven everywhere and were no longer able to ramble and explore as we had all done as children, were growing up with no knowledge of the feel of mud or the smell of ponds. So with the inspiration of a biology teacher who came to us with the idea, we opened the Field Centre, which is now the Field Centre Trust. We had always assumed that the education authority would help us with a salary. All the other counties had set up their own Field Centres and Suffolk was using our resources to educate 3,000 to 4,000 of their children in what are now National Curriculum subjects. But a salary was not forthcoming and ever since 1983, we have struggled with the shortfall between what the schools can afford and what it actually costs. We have a marvellous team of part-time teachers, a full time Head and an Administrator. The courses range from the tinies'; Key Stage 1 and 2, to sixth form self-led groups, team building, residential courses in the cabins we put up in 1986, farming and conservation and anything else we are asked for. We have recently developed courses on recycling, teambuilding and alternative energy.

We opened a small tea room, again to try to create jobs and somewhere for our walkers to recover from the mud they encounter almost all the year round on this heavy land. Over the years a lot of the local young people, including our grandchildren, have worked there in the summer months. Apart from the cream teas and coffee for our adult visitors, it provides mountains of fish fingers and burgers for the school children.

We have a camp site with very good washing facilities and another log cabin (as an addition to tents) which is used a lot in the summer, and, for many years by groups who came from a very deprived area in Islington.

We took part in the successive government schemes such as the Youth

Opportunities Programme, Youth Training Scheme and Community Programme until they were abandoned by government on the grounds that they were more expensive in the country and were better run by private effort in towns. The buildings that had been used in Thornham Street we eventually let to a group of disabled people who gradually established a woodwork workshop and IT training centre. This is now funded by social services and self help, and over the years we have helped with fund raising efforts to improve the buildings and facilities. Now in the year 2001, there are plans to expand more into horticulture. The tenants of our craft workshops too have changed; now in 2001, we have offices and IT businesses alongside the three craft workshops that remain. There are 16 units and enquiries come all the time. Rural business and working from home are expanding and the conversion of redundant farm buildings is a matter of course.

The Field Centre is run with enthusiasm and energy but funding is a continual problem. In the summer of 2000 we opened our Walled Garden which had taken five years to restore with grants from charities, ourselves, volunteer labour and a National Heritage Lottery Grant to rebuild the glasshouses. This marvellous place will enable us to offer courses in horticulture, mainly to people with disabilities, and provides us, and the community, with a place for concerts, exhibitions and celebrations.

We have we feel, almost finished the self imposed programme of restoration at Thornham. We now have good buildings, plenty of activity and opportunities for enjoyment and learning, and people working here with enthusiasm and energy. But I came to the conclusion some time ago that for a small private enterprise like ours, operating on its own, to expect to achieve its objectives or even to survive in an effective form has probably become an impossible pipe dream. I therefore thought that we must try to join or ally ourselves to some larger enterprise which has the same sort of objectives and is part of a wider world and a more established network, with access to a bigger infrastructure and to information, communications and official attitudes not automatically open to us. Being on our own outside the mainstream, without natural access to information or support, not only impairs our usefulness, but also, in educational activities and such matters as the care of children, is nowadays pretty dangerous.

I also thought that in respect of the provision of access and teaching

*Silver Wedding,
July 2001*

*below:
With all the
grandchildren.*

about conservation in this tiny area of north Suffolk, we should be more widely useful and more effective if we could make a partnership with the district council and become, instead of an isolated island in a fairly large area, part of the admirable network they seem to be building through the links between the Waveney, the Broads, the Breckland, the Gipping, the walks around Eye and such things as the lakes at Needham Market. We could add a bit to that. We have now and for the next 20 years a management agreement with Mid Suffolk District Council, which has taken a great load off our backs – not yet as much as we had hoped – again because money is so difficult to find in a countryside which is earning no money itself.

Over the years we have found and used our own capital to fund all this and charities have been an enormous help. But we begin to feel too old and exhausted to continue the constant struggle for funds to keep all these activities going and the infrastructures kept up.

We have established a strong and able management company and a board of trustees to manage and gradually take over from us. This involves our whole community in playing an active part, and we hope will provide insurance for its future.

Our only aim has been trying to help people in this part of the world to have a slightly fuller and more interesting life through the Estate than might otherwise be possible, and we have no other agenda, except to hope to keep this Estate as a going and lively concern and a thing of refreshment and beauty. We regard access to the countryside and education as the most important of our activities, for our aim is to offer the peace and tranquillity of the country to children, and also to those whose lives often contain a lot of extra worry and illness.

With the restoration of the Walled Garden, we feel that the main bulk of our enterprise has fought its way through with great difficulty, and must therefore – if it is to make a lasting contribution which it is well designed to provide – be kept going until some more permanent financial security can be achieved. We feel that we have so far been more successful than we expected and there must be a chance of maintaining momentum until Thornham has become fully part of the fabric of this beautiful county.

APPENDIX

History of the Thornham Estate and the Henniker-Major family

Thornham and the family
There is evidence of human activity in the Thornham landscape dating back to 2500 BC, and the continuity of this activity through to the present is remarkable.

The River Dove and the Roman road from Coddenham are important features, and their crossing is a constant point of interest.

During the Iron Age our area was a major landholding in the territory of the Iceni tribe, becoming part of the Villa Faustini estate under the Romans.

In the early Saxon period there was settlement near the river, expanding during the middle and late Saxon period when the church at Thornham Parva was built and there were links with Eye Priory. The Priory was one of the major landowners in the area, and in 1220 Abbott Anselm gave to Vitalis, who was one of his monks, land in Thornham for a hermitage: a chapel dedicated to St Arborys. There is a wealth of documentary evidence to show how the Estate became part of one of the largest landholdings in north Suffolk, totalling well over 30,000 acres in the nineteenth century.

From Norman to Tudor times
Doomsday Book records 52 people in Thornham Magna and 13 in Thornham Parva. One manor was held by a farmer called Isaac and another by Robert Malet who presented it to the Priory at Eye, whence it passed to the Crown and was given by Henry VIII to Charles Brandon, Earl of Suffolk, who had married Henry's sister Mary Tudor Queen of France, she was buried at Westhorpe.

Under Edward III the Estate was vested in William de Briseworth, and later passed to the Wiseman family. Thornham Hall was built in the sixteenth century when the Bokenhams followed the Wisemans. It is the tradition that Queen Elizabeth slept here on one of her East Anglian progresses. The chronicle records that "she lay at Thornham".

The churches
Records show that there were churches in Thornham Parva and Thornham Magna in the eleventh century. St Mary, Thornham Parva has wall paintings dating from the early thirteenth century. They are of great interest since they include one of only two surviving cycles in English wall painting of scenes from the life and death of St Edmund, King and Martyr. There is also a magnificent treasure dated about 1410 in this church – a retable discovered in the stables at Thornham in 1927. It is understood that another panel now in the Musee de Cluny, Paris, originally formed part of the same altar – probably the high alter of the Dominican priory at Thetford. St Mary Magdalen church at Thornham Magna was built in the fifteenth century. The fourth Lord Henniker restored it in 1851 with church furniture from the Great Exhibition.

The Killigrews and the arrival of the Majors and Hennikers
The Estate passed from the Bokenhams when Jemima Bokenham married Charles Killigrew. The Killigrews supported Charles I and followed Charles II to exile in the Netherlands. Robert Killigrew was Charles's representative in Venice and returned to England at the Restoration when he became Groom of the Bedchamber and, was variously known as the Master of the Revels or the King's Jester. As such he was responsible for reopening the theatre after its abolition under Cromwell and he himself wrote plays. Charles was his son as was General Robert Killigrew who was killed at Almanza in Spain in 1707 and has a memorial in Thornham Magna church. Charles Killigrew was succeeded at Thornham by his son Charles, who died without an heir in 1756. He bequeathed Thornham to his godson, the Rev. Charles Tyrell of Gipping, who sold it to Sir John Major.

Sir John Major
The Majors were reputed to be of French origin. Sir John Major was born in Bridlington in 1698. He was a merchant of the Muscovy company, a Director of the South Sea Company, Elder Brother of Trinity House, High Sheriff for Sussex 1755 and MP for Scarborough 1761. He was created a Baronet in 1756 with a special remainder to his son-in-law, John Henniker, 1784. Worlingworth Hall and Thornham were bought in 1756. Tradition also says

Sir John Major or perhaps a son who appears to have died on the voyage, accompanied Admiral Anson on his voyage round the world.

John Henniker

John Henniker married Ann – elder daughter of John Major in 1747, and was also a Russia merchant of the Muscovy Company, he lived at Rochester in Kent and was Freeman and merchant of that city. The Henniker origins are obscure; it is probable that they were descended from de Henkin, Governor of Dover Castle, but they may be Scandinavian, Onegar, from a village near Rochester. John Henniker was MP for Sudbury 1761-1768, and Dover 1774-1784. He succeeded to Sir John Major's baronetcy in 1761. Created Lord Henniker of Stratford upon Slaney, Co Wicklow in the Peerage of Ireland in 1800, he died in 1803.

Chandos connection

Both Major and Henniker were associated in business and in Parliament with James Brydges, who became first Duke of Chandos. Chandos began his career as Paymaster General and probably first had dealings with them in their capacity as merchants of the Muscovy Company who were importers of the white pine grown in Russia for the masts for the Royal Navy. Chandos was involved in a wide variety of entrepreneurial activities after retiring as the Paymaster General; he built a palace at Canons, Edgware, helped to develop Bath, Bridgewater, Harley Street, Cavendish and St James's Squares, Scotland Yard and Enfield and was in many other developments and speculative enterprises from the South Sea Company (with John Major) and the Africa, Levant and Muscovy Companies, to mining China clay. He died in 1744 having successfully offset his losses in his wilder enterprises with other successes, but the family fortunes declined under his heir and his great achievement – Canons – fell into disrepair. He was also a patron of Handel.

Elizabeth, second daughter of Sir John Major and heiress with her sister Ann, became the third wife of Henry second Duke of Chandos, in 1767 in an attempt to repair his fortunes. He died in 1771 and she spent much of her widowhood at Thornham Hall, which she earlier visited with the Duke. She brought Chandos pictures and other possessions to Thornham and shared the Estate with the first Lord Henniker (who had been widowed) as co-heir of Sir John Major. She died in 1813 at Major House (Thornham Hall). The Chandos connection is recalled by the names of the family and of various properties in and around the Estate, for example Duchess Wood and Chandos Farm.

The nineteenth century
The first Lord Henniker was succeeded by his eldest son, a Fellow of the Royal Society (as an antiquarian), a founder of the Royal Institution and also active in the Muscovy Company: his extensive Russian travels were recorded in his journal. In the Napoleonic Wars he raised a regiment of volunteers at Worlingworth and seemed to enjoy being painted in uniform. Like his father and his eventual successors – the first, fourth and fifth Lords Henniker – he was a Conservative MP and able as an Irish peer to sit in the House of Commons. He was MP for Romney 1785 to 1790, for Steyning 1794 to 1802, for Rutland 1805 to 1812, for Stamford 1812 to 1818. He married Emily Jones and died without heir in 1821. His only sister, Elizabeth, married the second Earl of Aldborough, who hoped by this means to acquire a sizeable income and repair his fortunes. He built Aldeborough House in Dublin. Thornham Hall was improved by adding the stables, designed by the architect Sidney Smirke.

The Third Lord Henniker, a cousin and son of Major, (the second son of the first Lord Henniker) succeeded. A lawyer, he married Mary Chafy, daughter of a Canon of Canterbury, who planted some of the woods, including Lady Henniker Wood. He took the additional name Major by deed poll. His son, John fourth Lord Henniker, was MP for East Suffolk 1832 to 1847 and 1858 to 1866 and High Sheriff for Suffolk 1853. He was active in the county, in parliament and in business, in promoting the railways, the Great Exhibition and the industrial development of the country.

He married Anna Kerrison, a daughter of General Sir Edward Kerrison of Brome Hall and Oakley Park – an important neighbour and landowner. She did much for the Estate. In 1866 he was created Lord Hartismere in the UK peerage and his elder son took over his parliamentary seat. He remodelled the Hall making additions to enhance its grandeur – building something on the lines of a French chateau between the two existing wings and including a grand Louis XVI saloon, adding towers and turrets and blocking out much of the light leaving the house colder and darker.

The household
The census of 1851 showed 26 people living at the Hall – six family, Lord Henniker, his wife and four children and 20 staff including a Swiss butler and his English wife who was also the housekeeper, a nurse and nursemaid, a stillroom maid, governesses (one of whom was French), gardeners, needle-women, a housemaid, four kitchen maids and a lady's maid, cook, labourer and two footmen who stoked fires in all the rooms.

The Estate and the family
When the fifth Lord Henniker succeeded his father in 1870 the Estate was in its heyday. There were 30,000 acres in Suffolk and probably more in Essex, Kent and Sussex. Disreali had foretold when the Corn Laws, which protected English agriculture, were repealed in 1849, that a flood of foreign produce would spell the end of English agriculture. But for some 40 years his prophecy was not fulfilled. Landowners and farmers continued in their old ways. At Thornham Lord Henniker and his wife who had been Lady Alice Cuffe, only daughter of the third Earl of Desart, raised a large family of 12 children. The house was constantly full of visitors. Lord Henniker had been sent to Cambridge as a friend of Edward VII and his fat and amusing sister Helen was popular with the King for her wit. He moved in circles, which included the best game shots of the period who often stayed at Thornham, the Princes Freddie and Victor Duleep Singh, whose guardian he was with Lords Ripon and Walsingham on Queen Victoria's behalf after their exile from India after the Mutiny. The family travelled regularly with all their retainers from Thornham to Worlingworth Hall and on to London where the season was spent at 6 Grafton Street. After succeeding his father and leaving the House of Commons he worked hard. He was in two of Disraeli's governments, a lord-in-waiting and junior minister in the House of Lords. He was first Chairman of the East Suffolk County Council – all jobs that were unpaid.

His children grew up at Thornham untroubled by the world with the standard careers of children of the aristocracy being mapped out for them. The house was always full of relations – many of them connected with the Cuffes (Lady Henniker's family) in Ireland.

People of the Estate
John Perkins was head gardener in 1883 when the Hall then had 25 acres of garden. He died in 1907. He was well known for his elaborate and elegant table decorations, on which he published a book, which was a minor classic of its kind.

There are no statistics of how many people worked outside Thornham Hall, but the Estate was unquestionably by far the largest if not the exclusive employer in the area; at one time as many as nine gardeners worked in the Walled Garden. One man was employed to flag down trains, which stopped at Thornham in return for Lord Henniker promoting the railway and allowing it to cross his land, and another was employed to supply fresh fish for the table. The stone folly, the ice-house, the Walled Garden and the model farm at the Red House, as well as the water tower, the pets' graveyard and the yew walks date from this period. The workshops at the Red House housed many Estate workers, cowmen and dairymaids, horsemen, carpenters and joiners, a wheelwright, woodmen and sawyers and gamekeepers of whom there were still seven until the 1930s.

People moved between the villages and beyond on foot. Today's footpaths show a well used system of paths used by most people to get to work, school, church or chapel, the pub or the mill near the Stoke Ash White Horse.

The family in the 1890s:
the decline and preservation of the present Estate

The eldest son, Bertie, a godson of King Edward, went to Australia to learn something of politics as Private Secretary/ADC to the Governor of New South Wales. The second son, Charles, joined the Rifle Brigade. The third son, Gerald, was destined to be a diplomat, but when the time came the family could no longer produce the money (£400 a year) which an aspiring diplomat was expected to have. The fourth, Victor Alexander, a godson of Queen Victoria, trained to become a parson and occupy one of the family's livings, while John, the youngest, was a page to Queen Victoria and earned enough to pay his school bills at Radley where his elder brother Victor had also been. The daughters, kept carefully to the bosom of the family, knew nothing of the world or its dangers, a lack of knowledge, which tended to prejudice their future happiness.

In the early 1890s Lady Henniker's diaries became very gloomy. The illness from which she died was approaching and economic difficulties were flooding in on her husband. Disreali's prophecy was now, 40 years later, coming home to roost. North America's transport and marketing systems had improved; steady streams of cheap corn were reaching British ports, while further afield Australia, New Zealand, South Africa and even Argentina were producing livestock efficiently and had mastered the problem of freezing meat. English agriculture was wilting under the strain and rents were impossible to maintain. For Thornham disaster came apace, and was the start of a decline in agriculture which, with short remissions before and during the First World War, went on through depression until the start of the Second World War. Other estates in the area declined more quickly. The Kerrisons disappeared and their successors – the Batemans – from Oakley Park and Brome Hall which were pulled down. At Redgrave the Holt Wilson's home, designed by Capability Brown, lasted until the Second World War before being pulled down. Lord Walsingham retired to the South of France and farmers and landowners fell into sore straits.

In 1892 Alice Henniker died and her husband, the fifth Lord Henniker, who had been a lord-in-waiting to Queen Victoria, was forced to seek a paid job under the Crown. In 1895 he was appointed Governor of the Isle of Man and remained there with many of his family until his death in 1902.

On his departure Thornham Hall was let. Six months before he died in 1902 his elder son, Bertie, had died suddenly of pneumonia. His heir, Charles, was with his regiment in India. Confusion reigned and from then until his nephew could return and his own death in 1912, the 5th Lord Henniker's younger brother, General Arthur Henniker, a guardsman, with his intellectual wife, Florence daughter of Lord Houghton and a close friend of Thomas Hardy, kept an eye on the Estate and the family. The children carried on as best they could. John, the future seventh Lord Henniker, was leaving school and it was decided that now that the family had no money, his best prospect would be to be trained as a Land Agent and eventually manage the Estate for his brother. He was sent to Cirencester. For the five remaining daughters the prospects were even more difficult.

The sixth Lord Henniker returned from India after a punitive expedition as part of the Afghan War, having decided that, with 10 brothers and sisters to provide for, he could not marry and must break off his engagement. He took his battalion to France at the beginning of the First World War. They had dreadful losses at Ypres and Arras on the Western Front and these disasters were a constant sorrow for the rest of his life. Debts were astronomical, there were death duties to pay as well, and these worries hung over his head until the end of his life. When the war was over, with the Hall leased to Colonel Hughes, he decided he must sell the greater part of the Estate; 21,000 acres were sold in 1919. This had to be repeated after the Second World War, when another 7,000 acres were sold leaving 3,000 acres of the original Estate.

In the mid-thirties the Hall's long-term tenant, Colonel Hughes decided to leave and, after all attempts to find another tenant had failed, it was decided to sell nearly all its contents (except pictures specifically involving the family) and to pull down the greater part of the house, which with no heating, no bathrooms and some 95 rooms was increasingly unmanageable. The remainder of the house was converted and pleasantly modernised by Guy Hake and the sixth Lord Henniker moved in. No sooner had he done so than it was requisitioned for an army HQ and Lord Henniker decided at the end of the war not to move again. The Hall was again let – to a school – and was burnt down in 1954. In 1956 Lord Henniker died and was succeeded in the title by his youngest brother, the seventh Lord Henniker who had returned in 1932 when the old Agent died to fulfil the plan originally made for him to manage the Estate. He and his family lived at the Red House and he continued to be closely involved with managing the Estate, which he successfully kept going, until his elder son returned in 1978 from a career in Diplomacy where he had been Ambassador to Jordan and Denmark and in the British Council as Director-General. The seventh Lord Henniker died at the age of 97 in 1980.

Modern day Thornham
After retiring from public service the eighth Lord Henniker was involved in charitable and voluntary work in London. He now lives at Red House, the old Agent's house. His aim has been to make the Estate of service to the community. He immediately opened it to the public with 12 miles of way-marked walks, which are today managed by the local authority. Agriculture was moving into another period of decline and local employment was shrinking. To help to ease this problem the obsolete buildings on the Red House Farm and its workshops were converted to provide workspace for employment and for people to set up small businesses.

In 1985 a Field Study Centre was opened to enable school children to use and learn about conservation and ecology on the Estate. All the courses are based on the National Curriculum. Accommodation for 28 people and a conference centre have been built.

The summer of 2000 saw the re-opening of the Walled Garden, restored with a combination of the family's money, charitable donations and with a National Heritage Lottery Grant for the eighteenth-century glasshouses. The Walled Garden now provides horticultural courses for students with disabilities and is a venue for lectures, concerts, weddings and other local activities.

The Estate is now, in 2001, run by trustees for the benefit of five grandchildren, who live in the rebuilt Thornham Hall.

The present Lord Henniker explained his aims after he inherited the title in 1980: "I had always thought that by sheer good luck I had the joy of owning a lovely place like this, I owed a duty to other people. I felt that as far as I could, I ought to try and share it with people, and to maintain and conserve its character and beauty."